Copyright @2021 by Peter King

All rights reserved. No part of this book may be reproduced in any form or by any electronic or mechanical means, including information storage and retrieval systems, without permission in writing from the publisher, except by reviewers, who may quote brief passages in a review.

This publication contains the opinions and ideas of its author. It is intended to provide helpful and informative material on the subjects addressed in the publication. The author and publisher specifically disclaim all responsibility for any liability, loss or risk, personal or otherwise, which is incurred as a consequence, directly or indirectly, of the use and application of any of the contents of this book.

WORKBOOK PRESS LLC
187 E Warm Springs Rd,
Suite B285, Las Vegas, NV 89119, USA

Website:	https://workbookpress.com/
Hotline:	1-888-818-4856
Email:	admin@workbookpress.com

Ordering Information:
Quantity sales. Special discounts are available on quantity purchases by corporations, associations, and others.
For details, contact the publisher at the address above.

ISBN-13:	978-1-956017-89-2 (Paperback Version)
	978-1-956017-90-8 (Digital Version)

REV. DATE: 11/03/2021

Has a very strong faith and knows that God's Grace has a lot to do with it. As well as being very positive and optimistic and trying to encourage people to believe in God, has learnt a fair bit over the years and is very rarely short of an answer when questioned about his faith. Knows that studying and learning about God's Grace is going to help a lot of people as well as himself. Has a lot of feelings for God's Grace and put's his heart and soul in to understanding and accepting it, and knows that God's Holy Spirit will be guiding him through it and throughout the rest of his life.

ACKNOWLEDGEMENTS

John & Dianne Johnson	I would like to thank both of them for leading my house group/bible study and teaching me nearly all I have learnt over the years
Pauline Evans, Anne Froud and Christine Coleman	Three people from my house group/bible study who have helped me with my studying and learning of God's word (the bible)

Rev. Brian Hall (St. Andrews Church, Gorleston) + Rev. Matthew Price, Rev. Trevor Riess and Rev. Peter Stephens (St. Mary Magdalene Church, Gorleston)	I would like to thank them all for their sermons at the various services they have done in the past and do in the future and for everything these sermons or talks have taught me about God's word (the bible)
members of the congregations at St. Andrews Church, Gorleston and St. Mary Magdalene, Gorleston	I would like to thank the people of these congregations for their help and support since the 1980's for helping me with my learning about God's word (the bible)
Linda Thompson	A previous member of my house group/ bible study who helped me with my studying and learning of God's word (the bible)

John Kinchin-Smith and Melvyn Reid	I would like to thank them for their sermons at the services they have done in the past and do in the future, and for everything these sermons or talks have taught me about God's word (the bible)
Bob French, Olive Wilson, Joan Tubby, David & Gill Norton, Tony & Rita Jaye + Dorothy & John McCabe	People who used to lead my house groups/bible studies in my early days of being taught God's word (the bible)
Roberta Lovick	A close friend and a Born Again Christian

THE POWER OF GOD'S GRACE

Chapter Titles

#	Title	#	Title
1	Creation	26	Peace
2	Birth	27	Health
3	Excitement, Joy & Elation	28	Healing
4	Positivity, Optimism & Inspiration	29	Glory
5	Happiness & Exaltation	30	Light of the World
6	Rejoicing	31	Holy Communion
7	Love	32	Devotion
8	Kindliness & Care	33	Blessed
9	Calmness & Relaxation	34	Harmony
10	Patience	35	Discipleship
11	Strength & Determination	36	Welcome
12	Motivation & Enthusiasm	37	The Trinity
13	Courage & Confidence	38	Friendship
14	Knowledge	39	Humbleness & Humility
15	Hope	40	Communication
16	Faith, Belief & Trust	41	Body, Soul & Spirit

17	Being Saved & Salvation	42	Presence
18	Eternal Life	43	Beauty & Nature
19	Justice	44	Sacrificing Life
20	Righteousness & Holiness	45	Conquering Death
21	Fearlessness	46	Freedom
22	Mercy	47	Sanctification & Consecration
23	Born Again	48	Magnifying & Magnification
24	Forgiveness & Repentance	49	Promises & Plans
25	Prayer		

CHAPTER 1

Creation

As part of his Grace God created the universe and created life. This included creating the heavens and the earth plus human mankind. Everything that takes place in this universe is taking place in what God created. Without the creation of this universe human mankind would not have been able to live their lives and because God created the universe we are all God's children. Born Again Christians are extremely thankful and grateful to God for his creation because they know their lives are important and special to both themselves and God. God created human mankind and promises and plans them to have perfect bodies. Born Again Christians know that due to the presence of Satan (i.e. The Devil) that their earthly lives will not be perfect because of sinning and health issues etc. but this is only a temporary thing. It may not seem temporary but life on earth is going to be temporary for all of human mankind. For Born Again Christians life in Heaven is going to be eternal and permanent. God creates all human beings and each has a choice to make and that is whether or not to have faith, belief and trust in him. Born Again Christians choose to have faith, belief and trust in him and they know that although they don't have perfect bodies during their earthly lives they will overcome this through their true faith, belief and trust in him. They know that when Jesus Christ returns, and due to his sacrifice on the cross (resurrection), they will be going to Heaven with him because they have been saved. This is all possible because of God's creation. God creating the universe is a massive thing and because he is in control of it all the time he knows who is with him and who is not plus who has faith, belief and trust in him and who doesn't.

For people who are not Born Again Christians and not likely to be so, understanding what God has created is going to be very hard and because of not understanding and accepting God's Grace. Because they have the presence of Satan (i.e. The Devil) with them and because he is taking control of people who are not Born Again Christians he is making them forget that God created the whole universe including their own bodies. They either have no idea or just want to reject the fact that God created the whole universe including their own bodies. Satan (i.e. The Devil) is putting negative thoughts and feelings in to people who are not Born Again Christians and trying as hard as possible for it to work, and unfortunately for non-believers they are letting him take control of them. The evil in Satan (i.e. The Devil) is making people who are not Born Again Christians take things including life for granted and expecting to receive whatever they want plus get their own way as well. God is creating and providing all of human mankind with a body and a life, and has promised them perfect bodies. For people who are not Born Again Christians they are not only rejecting that fact but they are also not realising that Jesus Christ sacrificed his life on the cross (resurrection) for them to be given a chance to live a life with a perfect body, which God promised. Unless a non-believer is converted to a Born Again Christian then their chance of having a perfect body and living a perfect life in Heaven will be non-existent. People who are not Born Again Christians don't realise how important it is and how much it should mean to all human beings to be created and be part of the universe that God has created. God goes above and beyond to love everyone but non-believers have no thought and feelings and are completely rejecting that they are one of God's children and part of his world.

Personally, for me, as well as being a Born Again Christian I am exceptionally thankful and grateful to God for his creation including creating me and giving me a life to live. I know that through his Grace God has promised me a perfect body and I know that although I have the presence of Satan (i.e. The Devil) during my earthly life my faith, belief and trust in God will overcome the presence of Satan (i.e. The Devil). Unfortunately for Satan (i.e. The Devil) he will eventually fail because he knows that my faith, belief and trust in God are too strong for him to get the better of me. God created me as part of his universe to have faith, belief and trust in him, live a life as a Born Again Christian, know that Jesus Christ as my saviour sacrificed his life on the cross for me, and to provide me with a perfect body and life. Satan (i.e. The Devil) tried to ruin and destroy my life on various occasions including when I had forty years of epilepsy and fifteen years of after effects after being diagnosed with cancer but through God's Holy Spirit being with me I managed to overcome Satan (i.e. The Devil). God knew that when he created me as one of his children I would overcome anything and be able to go a long way. He filled me with as much of his goodness as possible and knew that included love, hope, strength, motivation, faith and many other things. After the hard times I have experienced in the past God knew that if I had to face any more hard times I would be able to cope with them because of how he created me and wants me to be like. I want God's sanctification to be working on me throughout the whole of my life. When God created the universe he promised me a perfect body which will eventually happen, through Jesus Christ sacrificing his life for me and through my faith, belief and trust in him, throughout my daily life during my earthly life.

CHAPTER 2

Birth

For people who are Born Again Christians the birth of Jesus Christ is very important and means everything to them. As part of God's Grace the birth of Jesus Christ should be very important and special to every human being in this universe (past, present and future) but only Born Again Christians will know and understand how much it means. Without the birth of Jesus Christ, he would not have been able to sacrifice his life on the cross for all of human mankind so that they have a chance to live eternal life and a perfect life in Heaven. God's promise and plan includes providing all human mankind with a perfect life and that still exists today. God the Father knew that Satan (i.e. The Devil) would come along and exist at some time and prevent perfection on earth from lasting. That is the reason why the birth of our saviour Jesus Christ is so important and Born Again Christians celebrate his birth every year on what is called Christmas Day. Because Born Again Christians have faith, belief and trust in God they know that the birth of Jesus Christ is going to be a big thing in their lives because it will not only give them a second chance but they will be living the kind of life they should have been living if temptation and Satan (i.e. The Devil) hadn't existed. That is a perfect life and is what God still promises today. The difference between Jesus Christ being born and not being born is really massive. Without the birth of Jesus Christ, even those that have faith, belief and trust in God the Father would still have to live a life full of evil because of Satan (i.e. The Devil). As well as being born on 25th December and being born in Bethlehem he also came to preach the good news.

For people who are not Born Again Christians, have no intentions of being so, and have no faith, belief or trust in God their feelings for Jesus Christ and what his birth means will be near enough non-existent. The strength of Satan (i.e. The Devil) will be working on non-believers and people who are not Born Again Christians and putting negative thoughts and feelings in to them and deterring them from believing in the birth of Jesus Christ, and will make them think that it is all made up and just not true. Unfortunately for non-believers and people who are not Born Again Christians, having no faith, belief and trust in God will also mean they have no interest in the birth of Jesus Christ, and will make life harder for them and give them no chance of living a perfect life in Heaven. They will unfortunately be condemning themselves to a life in Hell a long with Satan (i.e. The Devil). Some Born Again Christians will be trying their hardest to help non-believers in understanding the truth about the birth of Jesus Christ, and what it all means, but a good majority will find it hard to convert to becoming a Born Again Christian. Most non-believers find it hard to accept both the birth and resurrection of Jesus Christ because their understanding is not the same as Born Again Christians and don't realise or want to know that the difference between what God promises them and where they will end up will be completely the opposite. Believing in the birth of Jesus Christ is a serious thing but for non-believers to ignore it and have nothing to do with it that is even more serious and will also have serious consequences to it. Non-believers and people who are not Born Again Christian should try and think a bit more when they are told about the birth of Jesus Christ.

For me, Jesus Christ's birth means a lot because if he hadn't been born my life would have been completely different and I would have had no chance of living a perfect life. Jesus Christ was born so that I as a Born Again Christian and also a sinner could have a chance to live a sinless and perfect life in Heaven as God has promised me. Jesus Christ birth is as important to me as is his death and resurrection because both are as important as each other. Because of Jesus Christ's birth I am able to study God's word (the bible) and find out about what I need to know. I am so grateful and thankful for what God has promised me and that includes Jesus Christ's birth which means such a lot because it means the difference between having the chance of living a perfect life compared to having to live a life full of evil. As a Born Again Christian I try and talk to some people who I know are non-believers about what Jesus Christ's birth means to me. Some listen and ask me to explain a bit more and some have no interest in listening any more. Knowing that Jesus Christ was born as part of God's plan, and to save my life, makes me feel so special, being one of God's children and knowing that is all for my benefit. My faith, belief and trust in God will continue forever and knowing that Jesus Christ has been born so that I can live a perfect life in Heaven makes the feeling inside me feel so wanted and fills me with so much hope as well. The fact that Jesus Christ was born for me is so important to me and makes my life every much easier every day. Thinking about what it means to have Jesus Christ in my life and what he has done for me gives me such a close and warm feeling plus helps me to think about how good my future is going to be once my earthly life is over. I have so much to look forward to because of Jesus Christ and his birth as part of God's plan, it is so vital. I can't ask for more than what Jesus Christ has done for me.

CHAPTER 3
Excitement, Joy & Elation

God's Grace includes many things including excitement, joy and elation. All the excitement, joy and elation within us, is provided by God because of his Grace. God's Grace is a free gift and is one of many gifts from our Lord. Although we all experience problems throughout our lives we are also filled with excitement, joy and elation. Certain events and certain things that happen to us during our lives fill us with excitement, joy and elation. It may happen to some of us more than others depending on how we live our lives and what happens to us. Sometimes we can make excitement, joy and elation in our lives, sometimes others fill us with excitement, joy and elation and sometimes things happen to us unexpectedly that fill us with excitement, joy and elation. Sometimes we are filled with excitement, joy and elation in a small way and sometimes in a big way. Some of us have excitement, joy and elation on a regular basis during our lives and some of us less often and only on exceptional occasions.

Those of us that accept God as our creator and those of us that are Born Again Christians are more likely to understand and accept God's Grace. Born Again Christians are also more likely to accept, be very thankful and be very grateful to God for his Grace. It means so much to us because it includes all the best things in life we can receive. He wants us to accept, receive and have as much excitement, joy and elation in our lives as possible. There is no limit to how much excitement, joy and elation God wants us to have.

For me, excitement, joy and elation, has featured quite a lot in my life, especially since I became a Born Again Christian. Sometimes it was birthdays and parties, sometimes other celebrations, sometimes winning competitions in lawn bowls and indoor bowls and sometimes it could be other things. The one thing that stands out for me is when I had my life saved when I was diagnosed with bowel cancer. When I was told I had bowel cancer I didn't get emotional or worried about it because the consultant had informed me before that, that he had saved my life and at that time all I could think of was being alive and being able tell people and carry on living. Internally the excitement, joy and elation got to me because it meant so much. I felt on top of the world because the difference between life and death is so massive. God was certainly talking to me, working on me and with me big time at that particular time. His Grace certainly filled me with excitement, joy and elation because he knew how much it would mean to me.

Although God's opposition Satan (i.e. The Devil) provided me with many years of pain after I was diagnosed with bowel cancer plus many years of pain of other kinds before it all happened the excitement, joy and elation of having my life saved will never leave me as it was such an important thing to me and it is not too likely to happen again. The excitement, joy and elation is there inside me all the time and also helps me to be so positive at other times.

For approximately forty years I also had to endure epilepsy, some bigger and some smaller seizures. That didn't make life easy, especially at school and when trying to apply for employment. The epilepsy started when I was four years-old in 1966 and I managed to grow out of it in 2006 when I was forty-four years-old. Later in 2006 I realised that my seizures no longer existed and I wasn't having them anymore and that gave me excitement, joy and elation on a slightly smaller scale than when I had my life saved after the cancer.

Since 1980 I have been involved in indoor and lawn bowls as part of my hobbies and interests. Over the years I have played many games/matches and had various results as well. It is always nice to win but taking part is just as important as well. In years gone by and in my first 10-20 years I may have been better at the indoor game and won a few trophies but in the past 20-30 years I have won a few more finals and trophies in the outdoor game. When you get to a final and when you win certain games/matches it can also give you a feeling of excitement, joy and elation. Although it is part of my life the excitement, joy and elation in playing bowls is not the same as having your life saved and being with God even though God is with me all the time.

Because of the various health problems, I have had due to mainly epilepsy and bowel cancer finding employment has been really hard for me ever since I first started job seeking in 1978, just before I left school. That could have easily affected me in a bad way but because of my positive outlook and faith I carried on searching and whenever I managed to obtain employment that gave me a feeling of excitement, joy and elation. I am still currently job seeking even though I am in my late fifties, and although they don't come too often I still get a sense of excitement, joy and elation whenever I can obtain an interview for a job. God always urges me to keep going and one day it will hopefully happen.

Another hobby and interest I have is cycling and that is only on a traditional bicycle, not a road racer. I am on the slightly slower side of cycling rather than the fast pace cyclists. Cycling is an everyday thing for me, as I have never had a driving license and a car; it becomes a regular thing for me. Not having to wait in traffic queues too often when I am on my bicycle makes it easier when I am out and about. As cycling is also part of exercising it also helps me in keeping on the move. Because I am living in God's world cycling, exercising and being on the move fills me with excitement, joy and elation as it is like freedom. Saying prayers while on the move is also possible.

CHAPTER 4

Positivity, Optimism & Inspiration

For a good majority of my life I have been positive, optimistic and inspirational, more so as I have got older. Receiving God's Grace means me being filled with positivity, optimism and inspiration. Having accepted God's Grace as a free gift to me means me putting what I have been given in to practice and using each part of God's Grace as part of my daily life. I am exceptionally thankful and grateful to my Lord for giving me positivity, optimism and inspiration and knowing that it is going to help me so much in my life. During my life so far I have met many people that have spoken and behaved in a negative way for different reasons and with my positivity, optimism and inspiration I have tried to help them as much as I possibly can. Being filled with positivity, optimism and inspiration can also be felt when going about my daily life as I don't ever look at a problem in a negative way, and that I immediately try and look for a solution without giving up. Being filled with positivity, optimism and inspiration makes life so different, especially compared to people who are so negative, those that give in to a problem and those who don't even try to make their lives more positive, optimistic and inspirational.

Having being filled with positivity, optimism and inspiration may have also helped me when I reacted to when I was diagnosed with bowel cancer and when I was told I had my life saved. It certainly helped me during all the years I endured a lot of pain with abdominal pain and adhesions, it also helped me during all the years I endured seizures when I had epilepsy. Whenever I have been job seeking it has helped me to keep going and never give up at any time. There have also been many other occasions in my life when I have needed to be positive, optimistic and inspirational so that I can cope with various things and overcome them.

Another thing that positivity, optimism and inspiration has done for me is it always makes me feel as if I am there for people who are feeling low and those who feel as if the world is against them. I have even spoken to people sitting in the streets plus homeless people and tried to offer them some positivity, optimism and inspiration. The same with other job seekers who feel there is nothing out there for them. Sometimes I offer positivity, optimism and inspiration to patients who have been through cancer and are suffering plus also people who are affected by seizures and epilepsy. I feel that being filled with positivity, optimism and inspiration by receiving God's Grace I am being used as one of God's disciples/servants to help others who don't have much positivity, optimism and inspiration in them.

The positivity, optimism and inspiration inside me each day really does give me a lift and makes me less likely to look out for problems, being negative and worrying. It makes me feel as if I can deal with the majority of things I am faced with in my daily life. Living with my parents throughout my life has also made me just as positive, optimistic and inspirational as my mum happens to be very pessimistic and negative. I often have to use my positivity, optimism and inspiration to prevent my mum being too pessimistic and negative. My dad is not quite so pessimistic and negative but I still do need to try and help him as well.

The positivity, optimism and inspiration inside me also makes me more outspoken and not frightened to discuss and talk about what I have been through and what I am still experiencing. Quite a lot of people are shy or fearful of discussing their experiences and problems, and don't like speaking about it but I am just the opposite. I was once involved in a cancer information group and was never frightened to speak out where necessary plus I also used to run a cancer support group and was the chairperson of that one. Both groups, due to the lack of numbers, have now finished. The support group lost people, more so because people were a bit nervous of speaking out too often. Because our personalities and ways are so different to each other, even if we have been through similar experiences, how we behave and how we react towards those experiences can be so different to each other. I have known people to get upset and be very emotional at being diagnosed with cancer, whereas I was excited at having my life saved even though I was also diagnosed with cancer. Sometimes the difference between being filled with positivity, optimism and inspiration as part of God's Grace can make all the difference.

Very often during my daily life if I am in conversation with someone and they happen to be talking about something and they eventually talk about something in a negative way I very often try and turn the conversation round by using my positivity, optimism and inspiration to say to the person that whatever they are speaking about is not as bad as they say because talking negatively won't help and they shouldn't give up on whatever it is they are talking about. Sometimes it is not easy to make people feel more positive, optimistic and inspirational but sometimes it can go a long way to helping people. If people are very pessimistic and negative giving them positivity, optimism and inspiration can even help them to make progress and talk and behave less negatively and not to give up on situations.

CHAPTER 5
Happiness & Exaltation

Our lives all include ups and downs, good times and not so good times, even bad times but due to receiving God's Grace we can still be happy and exalted throughout our lives. Sometimes excitement, joy and elation plus positivity, optimism and inspiration go a long way to being happy and exalted. Passions, hobbies and interests also help us to be happy. We ourselves can also make our lives happy and exalted by how we behave and go about things during our daily lives. How we react to various situations can also make a difference to us and that can be the difference between being happy and being sad or unhappy.

How others behave towards us, what people say and what people do during our lives can also make a difference between happiness and sadness. Taking things to heart or taking them the wrong way when we are spoken to in an inappropriate way can make a big difference in our lives as well. Because of my positive attitude to life if people try to speak to me in an appropriate way or they say something to me I don't agree with I just let them know once and don't get in to an argument or a long debate. I just let them know that the subject is over and finished with. People who do take things to heart and argue and debate things for a long time can find themselves getting irritated, stressed, angry and very unhappy. It may lead to friendships and relationships disappearing and nobody wants that to happen. Avoiding arguments and debates plus stopping an argument or debate once it has started would help a lot and be the difference between being happy or unhappy.

God's opposition Satan (i.e. The Devil) is the one who wants us all to be sad and unhappy because he loves to see people argue, debate, get emotional, fall out and hate each other for the rest of our lives. None of us want that and if we can avoid it as much as we possibly can it will help us so much. God, on the other hand, wants us all to be happy throughout our lives and be able to communicate in an appropriate way and make life as easy as we possibly can. If our lives were to run smoothly all the time the happiness and exaltation inside us would be with us all the time and that is something we do need. The happiness and exaltation inside us that comes from God's Grace is there all the time but how much we accept it, use it and put it in to practice is up to us. What we do ourselves can make us happy and exalted, and what others do to and for us can also make us happy and exalted but we must remember that it all comes from God's Grace which is a free gift from our Lord.

God's Grace which includes a free gift of happiness and exaltation can be used every day of our lives and how we deal with that is up to us. We all need to think during our daily lives, whether it is at home, at work, at school, out and about or in any other situation we may be in. How we speak and behave towards people is so important for us and others to be happy and exalted and to stay that way. Everyone's happiness and exaltation is important and we ourselves need to show that we intend to and are keen to see that everyone we come in contact with stays as happy and exalted as when we see them or becomes happier when we see them. We, ourselves, need to make others happy and exalted, and use God's free gift throughout our lives. Others will hopefully be the same to us but whether they have accepted God's Grace and understand that they have been given happiness and exaltation will be up to them and remains to be seen by us. Every day we discover how happy and exalted people are and how they deal with what they face during their lives.

During the forty years I was suffering with seizures when I had epilepsy, during the fifteen years I suffered with abdominal pain and adhesions plus a twisted colon after the bowel cancer, and during the many years of unemployment I have been through, it has never stopped me being happy and exalted. During all those years God's Grace and the gift of happiness and exaltation he provided me with was with me and never left me. It is still with me to this very day and always will be. With the exception of my early years of having epilepsy, when I was still at school, I realised that the suffering I was going through and the hard times I was going through all came from Satan (i.e. The Devil). He thought that he would be able to make me unhappy and that my life would never get any better and that it would make me totally unhappy throughout the rest of my life. At the same time God knew that he had given me his free gift of his Grace and that he had filled me with happiness and exaltation, and that whatever happened in my life

I would be able to deal with it and it would never be able to stop me being as happy and exalted as I have always been. Anyone who accepts God's Grace and is filled with happiness and exaltation will always be able to deal with whatever they face during their lives and still carry on being happy and exalted throughout their lives. How we deal with suffering and hard times throughout our lives is up to us but if we can try and find a solution ourselves or get help and support as soon as possible it will help us in our happiness and exaltation, and should not affect us too much. If we can't handle suffering and hard times throughout our lives, then we are letting Satan (i.e. The Devil) get to us and making us unhappy. Think about what the gift of God's Grace, plus happiness and exaltation has provided you with and means to you. Don't let anyone make you unhappy.

CHAPTER 6

Rejoicing

For Born Again Christians to be able to rejoice in what God has provided them with through his Grace is a wonderful thing and something to look forward to every day during their earthly lives. To be able to rejoice in something that God has provided Born Again Christians with is such a wonderful feeling. The fact that God the Father created the universe including all of mankind, God the Son (Jesus Christ) died on the cross for our sins and God the Holy Spirit is guiding us throughout our earthly lives is something Born Again Christians rejoice in on a regular basis, if not every day. There are many other things that Born Again Christians rejoice in every day during their earthly lives and they include the gifts that God has provided them with, good health, healing, being saved, having eternal life etc. God wants Born Again Christians to be able to rejoice in him as much as possible. Being thankful to God and being glad about something that God had to do with is also another way of being able to rejoice in God. Born Again Christians have small things happen to them during their lives, they also have big things happen to them during their lives, and some of those things are things they want to rejoice in because of God being part of their lives. For a Born Again Christian to be able to convert a non-believer in to being a Born Again Christian through magnifying God's Word (the bible) to them, during their earthly lives, that would be another thing a Born Again Christian could rejoice in because as one of God's disciples they would have done what God wanted them to do. To Born Again Christians their soul and spirit are very important to them, very precious and mean a lot to them, and that is another reason to rejoice in what God has provided them with.

For non-believers and people who are not Born Again Christians rejoicing in God's name will mean nothing and will be impossible because to them he hasn't provided them with anything and didn't create them. Satan (i.e. The Devil) is trying his hardest and very often succeeding with non-believers and people who are not Born Again Christians to make sure they don't rejoice in God or for anything God provides or does. Satan (i.e. The Devil) wants non-believers and people who are not Born Again Christians to rejoice in him and that means the enjoyment of bad thoughts, bad words, bad deeds and anything that can harm someone or something. Rejoicing in profiting in or gaining money or goods legally or illegally is another thing Satan (i.e. The Devil) wants non-believers and people who are not Born Again Christians to do. Satan (i.e. The Devil) knows that the majority of non-believers and people who are not Born Again Christians don't realise that he is trapping them in to rejoicing in sinning and creating bad and evil in the world. Every day there are non-believers and people who are not Born Again Christians sinning and rejoicing in it because Satan (i.e. The Devil) is getting to them, making life harder for them and they are unable to do anything about it because they are not with God. Rejoicing in sinning and anything bad and evil is not only going to let non-believers and people who are not Born Again Christians downfall but failure to be with God will mean being with Satan (i.e. The Devil) and ending up in Hell. The difference in rejoicing in something connected with what God wants people to have/do and rejoicing in something Satan (i.e. The Devil) want people to have/do is as big/massive as you can possibly imagine. They are completely opposites and extremes in what will happen to them and where they will end up.

As a Born Again Christian, I have many things to rejoice in and all through the Grace of God. The experiences of having forty years of epilepsy, fifteen years of bowel cancer and long periods of unemployment are just three things I have been able to rejoice in because God has got me through them and has been able guide me through all those years through his Holy Spirit. The bowel cancer experience also included having my life saved, and that is an additional and special thing for me to rejoice in. They were hard times but God's Holy Spirit filled me with strength, determination, motivation, positivity etc. and many other things that have given me in my soul cause to rejoice and be glad for everything God has done for me. Being able to attend church services and bible studies/house groups since the 1980's has been another thing I rejoice in doing because I am not only worshipping God but I am learning and studying his word. In my early days of studying God's word, it was harder but as time has gone by it has become easier for me. As well as growing in knowledge about God's word (the bible) I am also getting closer to God and so is my friendship with God, and they are things I am able to rejoice in. Magnifying God's word (the bible) to others is something else I rejoice in and as a disciple and one of God's children it is something as a Born Again Christian I need to do for others benefits so they can learn about God's word (the bible) and be saved, and eventually live a life in Heaven and not Hell. If the person/people, I magnify God's word to want to listen to me or not it is up to them. Being able to support people including my parents, look after them and love them at the same time is something else I can rejoice in because it is all part of love that God has given me, shows me and wants me to use as much as possible. Being able to rejoice in somebody or something is a wonderful and a wonderful feeling.

CHAPTER 7

Love

Another free gift and a big part of God's Grace is Love. Born Again Christians are all filled with love as part of God's Grace and how they go about showing it or not showing it is up to them. Some people are able to show it more than others and sometimes it depends what is happening in their lives and how things and other people affect them during their lives. Because Satan (i.e. The Devil) is trying to prevent them showing love towards each other some people will not realize that he wants them to show no feelings at all and even hate others including when problems occur between people which include arguments and disagreements. God, on the other hand, wants Born Again Christians to show love plus affection towards other people all the time, whatever situation we are in.

Putting it in to practise is one thing everyone needs to do because it will not only make our own lives a lot easier, it will also make everyone else's lives a lot easier. When people are showing love towards each other they want the best for each other in life and for each other to receive as much support in life as they need. Being close to people and having as much friendship towards people is also part of loving people. Strong relationships between two people as friends is also showing love. These relationships and friendships should be able to continue forever as long as they carry on loving each other. God wants the love between everyone to continue forever and carry on being as strong as possible between each other. Making friends and for friendships to be very close and to stay very close forever is showing love and that is one thing that God wants for us throughout the whole of our lives. He wants the best outcome for everyone and showing love towards each other is a massive thing in everyone's lives.

Because of the love within God's Grace, many people have shown love towards me and vice versa. My parents, who I have lived with throughout the whole of my life so far, have shown love to me since the day I was born. Both parents show their love towards me in slightly different ways though. My brother and his wife plus my niece and her children, and my nephew and his children have also shown love towards me throughout my life. People at my local church(s), people at my local outdoor bowls plus other clubs, people at previous indoor bowls clubs, people from places where I have been a volunteer plus people from other clubs and organisations have all shown love towards me over the years and still carry on doing so. I love them all and I will receive the same back. The sentence in the bible "LOVE THY NEIGHBOUR AS THYSELF" is very important. The staff in the hospitals I have attended for various reasons have shown their love towards me even though it was their jobs. Even if we are around strangers or people we know very little about we can still show love towards them because it is all important. If we show love towards others we should hopefully receive love back again. It should work both ways. If people bond together and the love and friendship is exceptionally strong and close that is a wonderful thing because that is all part of God's plan through receiving his Grace.

During my life so far I have been through some hard and difficult times but during those times I have always been shown love by everyone around me. How people have spoken to me, how they have treated me and the kind of feeling I get when people show their love towards me is wonderful and that is all coming from God's Grace. During both the forty years I suffered with epilepsy and during the fifteen years I suffered with the bowel cancer plus the after effects of it I was shown love by quite a lot of people from family and neighbours to hospital staff in both the UK and USA and people from my church(s), bowls clubs and where I do volunteer work. All the people that have shown love towards me in the past, at the present time and in the future I have and will intend to show love towards because it is part of what God has given to me to put in to practise and part of his Grace.

Showing genuine love towards people through God's Grace is usually recognisable through how people go about their daily lives, how they speak, communicate and behave towards others, and that it should continue forever if it is genuine and true love. If it starts off as so called love or what seemed like love, between two or more people, and then starts to disappear by differences, arguments and bad feelings occurring then it is not genuine love and is not coming from God's Grace. Satan (i.e. The Devil) will be invading at that time and may prevent people showing genuine love and if they let him get his own way love will be harder for them to show and put in to practise as well. For those people, genuine love will need some working on and they will need help, praying for and possibly need to know more about what love really is and that is all comes from God's Grace. The difference between showing genuine love, love that you can feel, and love that is not genuine is really massive. If we want to be loved by everyone and we want to genuinely show love to others we need the love that come from God's Grace and is a free gift from our Lord throughout our lives. We also need to pray for God's Grace among other things and we also need to pray that other people receive God's Grace so that love is in everyone all the time.

CHAPTER 8
Kindliness & Care

Another thing we receive as part of God's Grace and God wants us to put in to practise throughout the whole of our lives is kindliness and care towards each other. How we speak, communicate and behave towards each other will determine whether we are showing kindliness and care towards each other. Because God's Grace is a free gift we need to pray so that we can carry on receiving it and the more we receive it God will provide us with it so that we can show our kindliness and care towards each other throughout our lives, and that will be noticed and should hopefully continue forever. God himself knows when we genuinely show kindliness and care towards each other. If we ourselves show kindliness and care towards each other then we should receive it back from those who we show it to. If we show it throughout our lives, then that should make life for everyone a lot easier.

The kindliness and care we show towards each other throughout our lives can be for many different things, in many situations and at any time. There are no restrictions on when we can show kindliness and care towards each other, God wants us to show it whenever we need to and at all times. There is no limit. Even praying is a form of kindliness and care because the thoughts during the prayer are for someone, maybe several people, and the thoughts come from the soul of the person or people praying and is showing kindliness and care for whoever they are praying for. We, ourselves, could be at home, at work, out and about shopping, taking part in a leisure or sport activity, visiting someone at home or in hospital, travelling around on road, rail, river or air, or in any other situation but whichever one of these situations we are in, if we have other people with or near us, it doesn't stop us showing kindliness and care towards them.

The kindliness and care that we show and comes from receiving God's Grace will come naturally to us if we are genuine when we show kindliness and care towards everyone we come in contact with during our daily lives. Satan (i.e. The Devil) will however try and prevent people showing kindliness and care towards others during their lives and that leads to people not being so kind or caring and showing bad feelings at times. Disagreements, arguments and falling out with someone can cause people to be not so kind or caring towards other people. This is something we don't need at any time during our lives, and also something that we can prevent happening as well. How we speak, communicate and behave towards each other is one factor as is how others react to us. The kindliness and care that is in our souls together with the thoughts in our minds need to blend together and will help us in what we say if and when we react to someone who is being unkind to us or being unpleasant as well. If someone tries to start a debate, argument or gets annoyed and aggressive we need to try and not react at all or let them know that they need to stop, and that the debate or argument is going no further plus the subject is over. If you react to someone trying to start a debate, argument or getting annoyed and aggressive in the wrong kind of way, and it gets out of hand that could lead to two or more people not being so kind and caring towards each other for quite a while or forever.

One thing about showing kindliness and care towards others is that it could even lead to new friendships because of people knowing how kind and caring we are and know that because of our personality and how we treat people they have nothing to worry about when they approach us. That is something that we all need in life and showing that kindliness and care is in us all because it is part of God's Grace. We also need the intention in our daily lives of being kind and caring, and we need to keep working on it whoever we come in contact with and however they approach us. If we believe and know that we are receiving God's Grace, then the kindliness and care inside us should make it a lot easier for us to put it in to practise.

I have been shown a lot of kindliness and care in my life so far, and that has come from many people including my family (especially mum and dad), friends from church(s), friends from bowls clubs, friends from various volunteer jobs, friends and colleagues from previous employment and staff from hospitals in the UK and USA. There are many more as well. I am also very grateful and thankful to all the people in my life that have shown me kindliness and care, and I hope that continues for the rest of my life. In return, I have shown kindliness and care to others during my life so far and I intend to carry on doing so in the future. There are particular times when people have shown exceptional kindliness and care towards me, and those stick in my mind for a long time. Sometimes it was part of someone's job and sometimes it came naturally to relatives and friends. If people show kindliness and care towards others more often during their lives the more they will be able to put it in to practise and eventually it will come naturally. Once we accept God's Grace the kindliness and care will be working in us more and more, and that is one thing we want and God wants us to be putting in to practise all the time

CHAPTER 9

Calmness & Relaxation

During our lives, whatever situation we are in, we always need to keep calm and relaxed. As part of God's Grace we are filled with calmness and relaxation but we have to put that in to practise for it to work. Sometimes we are put in to situations where it is harder to stay calm and relaxed and sometimes situations we are in happen very suddenly and they also make it harder for us to stay calm and relaxed. Calmness and relaxation is something we need to work on and put in to practise every day because things happen all the time, some unexpectedly. If people accept God's Grace, they need to realise that calmness and relaxation is very important in their lives and God wants us to stay calm and relaxed throughout our lives at all times and in all situations. Sometimes, in extreme situations in life, people are in situations where they are finding it very hard to stay calm and relaxed, and that their anger, frustration and bad feelings are shown, plus the thought of calmness and relaxation doesn't enter their thoughts and minds. Unfortunately, Satan (i.e. The Devil) enters their thoughts and minds and takes control of what they are thinking and saying, plus the wrong kinds of words come out and are very often offensive at times. Working on how to keep calm and relaxed takes a lot of doing but if Born Again Christians persist in trying during their daily lives it will eventually work. Preventing anger, frustration and bad feelings is one thing we need to do to keep calm and relaxed, as is trying to prevent ourselves becoming nervous and anxious about things. Unfortunately, Satan (i.e. The Devil) will also try to make us nervous and anxious during our lives. That too needs working on and if we want to stay calm and relaxed through God's Grace we need to think to ourselves before reacting to things in a negative way including being nervous or anxious. Even situations such as being far too excited and overjoyed can cause people to get out of control and have a problem with staying calm and relaxed. Big events and celebrations are big examples of this sometimes happening to people.

Because we need to stay calm and relaxed throughout our lives there are many more situations we can be in and show anger, frustration and bad feelings or we are nervous or anxious. Calmness and relaxation is something we need in us every day throughout our lives but each of us deals with it in a different way and for some of us it is fairly easy to keep calm and relaxed but for others it is much harder. If we want to stay calm and relaxed, we need to accept God's free gift of his Grace and realise that he wants us to stay calm and relaxed throughout our lives. Being able to keep calm and relaxed throughout our lives will help us so much and will help us in all walks of life, wherever we maybe.

During a good majority of my life so far I have nearly always been able to keep calm and relaxed in most situations and react to people and things in a calm and relaxed way. God's Grace is with and in me because my Lord wants me to stay calm and relaxed throughout my life. God is using me as one of his disciples and servants to stay calm and relaxed and if need be try and help others to stay calm and relaxed. If someone ever starts using anger, frustration and bad feelings towards me I usually let them say what they want to say and just stay calm and relaxed and then try and calm the other person down by talking to them in a calm and relaxed manner and ask them if they can calm down and talk normally.

There have been a few times during my life when I have been slightly nervous, not anxious though, but the majority of the time I stay calm and relaxed in most situations. Because God is with me all the time his presence in me helps me so much and that also removes most of the nervousness and anxiety out of me. It is only Satan (i.e. The Devil) who wants me to be nervous and anxious but God's Grace is much more powerful. To be able to keep calm and relaxed in most situations is a wonderful feeling because it makes life so much easier as well. Living with my parents throughout my life and being a single person also helps me with this situation as well. Having no wife and no children for me has made it easier and having fewer problems occurring. Leading a quieter life can mean staying calmer and more relaxed.

I have been and still am involved many things during my life and when I am involved these various things I have to stay calm and relaxed. I have been involved in the following things: - lawn bowls, indoor bowls, church services, house group meetings (bible studies), cycling, voluntary work, fundraising events, training courses, job clubs etc. Some of them I am still involved in and some I am no longer involved in. Doing training course examinations and being a jobseeker means having job interviews from time to time and in both cases that means staying calm and relaxed. Attending dentist, doctors and hospital appointments also means staying calm and relaxed as well. As I am living with my parents I am now at an age where I am looking after them as much as they are for me. They need help and support and that means me also staying calm and relaxed. Receiving God's Grace throughout my life helps me so much including in all the situations where I have needed to and will need to stay calm and relaxed. Staying as calm and relaxed as we possibly can throughout our lives is so important.

CHAPTER 10

Patience

God also gives us patience as part of his Grace and he wants us to have it and put it into practise throughout our daily lives. This is also a big part of how we conduct ourselves and behave during our lives. People that believe in and accept God's Grace and know that it is a free gift from him, will know that it includes the patience he wants us to have and the closer we are to God it will work for us. The stronger our patience is it will be easier for us to show it during our daily lives. Satan (i.e. The Devil) will try and make us as impatient as he possibly can and will try and test us as much as he possibly can. If we remember this, it may even help us when we are in situations when we need to be patient. People that don't understand or accept God's Grace will find it harder to realise that it is so important because we need it all the time and every day of our lives. Those people are being trapped by Satan (i.e. The Devil) and when it comes to having patience they are going to struggle and have either very little or no patience at all. That will also make life harder for them as well. Nobody wants that. Having no patience or very little patience when going about anyone's daily lives will make things exceptionally hard especially when it comes to communicating with other people. Any slight difference of opinion or a difference in reacting to what someone has said or done can make the difference between being patient and being impatient.

During my own life there have been many occasions when I have needed to be patient with other people and in many situations. During the forty years I was affected by epilepsy I had to be patient when having seizures, other people had to be patient with me as well. During the years I had the bowel cancer, abdominal pain and adhesions plus the twisted colon I also had to be patient, as did others with me. Since the day I finished school in 1979 it has never been easy for me to obtain employment and during that time I have also had to stay patient and keep trying. When I am participating in outdoor and indoor bowls games I have needed patience on the various club greens, and when I am cycling up the road most days or in charity bike rides I very often have to have patience as well. Because I have lived with my parents throughout my life and still do, I have to stay patient with them as well. They have also had to be patient with me, more so when I was a child. Because I know that God has given me his Grace as a free gift that also includes him providing me with many different things including patience. That thought sticks in the mind when going about my daily life as does when I am putting in to practise. When you have the intention of being patient with people and in situations it will usually work. Even people and situations that try and test your patience won't be able to because you are able to stay patient and cope with it.

The feeling of God's Grace working in us throughout our daily lives is not only a wonderful thing but it means we are closer to him and when patience is part of it the feeling of it working means we are in control of our patience and we think about more and more. When we are in conversation with other people we are able to stay patient whatever the subject maybe about, whoever we are in conversation with and wherever we maybe. If I ever notice the person or people I am in conversation with getting impatient I just say to them about finishing the conversation and forgetting the subject before it goes any further, so it prevents any more impatience on their part.

During my daily life I see many people displaying patience and impatience, some in similar places. When I have been shopping and people are waiting in a queue it certainly tests their patience. Some people will only wait a few seconds or minutes before they start losing their patience but others like myself are able to wait for as long as need be. Another place that tests people's patience is on the roads and I have very often witnessed drivers who have very little or no patience when they are on the roads, some of them passing me on my bike. Other drivers have a lot of patience and have to wait in queues for a long time, sometimes hours. Having patience or not having patience can be the difference between being safe and causing an accident, especially on the road. There have many situations I have witnessed where people just haven't got patience in general and can't wait because they require things to be done or things to happen instantly. Waiting or being patient is something they just can't manage. Those people need help and don't realise that someone is controlling them and preventing them having patience. Personally, I am someone who has a lot of patience, possibly too much sometimes. That is a good thing though. God is looking after me. Instead of always wanting to be first, in a hurry or unable to wait, people need to be more thoughtful in how they conduct themselves or behave during their daily lives and prevent themselves from becoming impatient, sometimes extremely impatient. Anyone who is willing to wait, sometimes for a long period of time, anyone who takes their time, and anyone who is able to conduct themselves and behave themselves in any situation has a lot of patience and with God's Grace will be able to control themselves for a long time, and hopefully forever.

CHAPTER 11
Strength & Determination

One thing all humankind needs is strength and determination and through receiving God's Grace Born Again Christians will have this in themselves. Everyone needs strength and determination at some time during their lives, some people quite a few times during their lives. Because God's Grace is a free gift the strength and determination, as part of it, is in Born Again Christians and whenever they need to put it into action they can do. Like all the other things within God's Grace strength and determination is so important. Born Again Christians accept and understand the gift of God's Grace and will realise that when they require it and need to put it in action strength and determination will feature in their lives quite often. The thought of strength and determination, as part of God's Grace, throughout people's daily lives will be very useful and will help people in many situations, good or bad. Satan (i.e. The Devil) will try and prevent people in accepting and understanding God's Grace plus will try and make us forget about having strength and determination, which will make it disappear out of our minds and when it comes to requiring strength and determination it won't be there in us. Satan (i.e. The Devil) will also try and make us as weak as he can and that will make life very hard. The difference between believing in God and receiving his Grace, and not, which means wanting Satan (i.e. The Devil) to control your life is massive. Not believing in the one and only God means you are against him and with Satan (i.e. The Devil).

Being a Born Again Christian and being with God all the time has helped me in many ways. Receiving God's Grace for me is a big thing including receiving strength and determination. I have required strength and determination on many occasions in the past and will possibly do so in the future as well. During the forty years I was affected by epilepsy I certainly needed strength and determination. Although the seizures were quite serious during my school days, as I got older they gradually got less serious and became a lot milder. Having strength and determination in me helped me so much in knowing how to try and overcome each of these seizures and also when reacting as I felt a seizure coming on. It also helped me assure other people not to worry when they saw me having a seizure. Many school children had no idea of what was happening when I had seizures. It didn't matter whether it was a minor or major seizure I still required strength and determination, and as I got older the inner strength helped me remember things a bit better. Epilepsy often makes people have memory loss as well. I eventually grew out of it in 2006 at the age of forty-four.

Having bowel cancer together with having abdominal pain and adhesions plus a twisted colon meant I really needed strength and determination to cope with it, overcome it and eventually beat it. The levels of pain and agony I was in during the years I was affected by abdominal pain and adhesions were extremely variable and went from very dull and low level pain to very high and severe level pain. The strength and determination that is in me and was during the years I was affected by this was there all the time and helped me to find a solution to make my situation better and improve things. I had to find ways to keep moving, exercise and find ways to keep the mind active and stop thinking of the pain and agony as much. I used to go walking, cycling, playing bowls, attending church and just keep busy in general as ways of keeping my mind and body active. The strength and determination made me force myself and push myself to overcome the pain and agony I was experiencing. It also helped me to keep control of myself and not get emotional, in fact the strength and determination that God has given me helped to realise how important having my life saved is. The strength and determination was and is also necessary because of having to give up particular foods due to causing problems with my internal body and causing more pain and agony if I did go against what I have been told by a professional dietitian.

Strength and determination has also helped me over the years when trying to obtain employment and finding it very hard. I have applied for thousands of jobs since I first starting doing applications in November 1978. Some have replied, more so in years gone by, but the majority haven't replied and still don't. The majority of my employment has been short term and seasonal jobs. Doing voluntary work has helped me as has having a few hobbies and interests. I have had quite a few job interviews over the years as well but with over 75% of them I have had negative replies and rejections, some no reply at all. With strength and determination in me I didn't let it worry me and had to carry on applying for jobs. Without strength and determination things would have been completely different for me. I have seen and witnessed for myself people that have been affected by unemployment and have reacted to it completely different to how I have. Whether or not they understand God's Grace and have strength and determination is hard to tell but reacting to being unemployed in a negative way means Satan (i.e. The Devil) is going to be testing them. If their situation goes from bad to worse, it could be that Satan (i.e. The Devil) is going get the better of them and make them a weak person. If it is only a short term problem and they are able to cope with being unemployed then God's Grace should hopefully be working in them and their strength and determination will be working as well.

The Power of God's Grace

CHAPTER 12

Motivation & Enthusiasm

Motivation and enthusiasm are also a big part of God's Grace and he wants Born Again Christians to be filled with as much of them as possible. Motivation and enthusiasm can really affect us and the more we have in us the more likely we are to be very keen on doing something and taking part in our interests, hobbies and passions even more so. It can help us in our daily lives and if we accept and understand God's Grace the motivation and enthusiasm will work in us. It will show how we feel and how keen we are at wanting to do something or take part in something. We can also be filled with motivation and enthusiasm in wanting to be at work or even wanting to meet someone. Another example would be if you are having a hard time in life but you are filled with motivation and enthusiasm and it makes you keen on coping with and overcoming that situation, plus beating that problem altogether. The more motivation and enthusiasm you are filled with you are going to be more willing to try harder at something and be extremely keen on doing or being involved in something. Being filled with motivation and enthusiasm through God's Grace should mean you won't let anything stop you from taking part in something or doing what you are going to do because it means so much to you and you are very keen. Motivation and enthusiasm are also part of being keen and wanting to pray at any time in our lives and in whatever situation we are in.

People who are non-believers and not Born Again Christians, and are not understanding and accepting God's Grace will mean Satan (i.e. The Devil) preventing any of them from being filled with motivation and enthusiasm, which could mean having very little or no motivation and enthusiasm at all. People who have been having a hard time and finding it hard to get going may struggle when they have no idea of God's Grace or not wanting to accept God's Grace. Not being filled with motivation and enthusiasm could possibly lead people to getting bored, being unable to make decisions plus finding it hard to do things and join in with different things. They will possibly struggle when it comes to being asked to do something and to do a favour for someone. It could also mean always declining things, having a negative attitude in life and not wanting to help themselves or seek help as and when they require it. With very little or no motivation and enthusiasm people will find life in general harder. Some people just have no intention of understanding and accepting God's Grace and will find Satan (i.e. The Devil) invading their lives and will prevent them ever having motivation and enthusiasm in their lives. It may not be the end of the world but with motivation and enthusiasm it should make life easier, depending on each individual's situation.

There have been many times when I have been filled with motivation and enthusiasm including when I participate in bowls matches and charity events. I also feel it when I am involved in voluntary work which includes meeting the general public and a lot of administration work. I feel it when I am applying for jobs and attending job interviews. In each of these situations I am keen to do well and even do my best and that is because of the motivation and enthusiasm that God has filled me with as part of his Grace. Being outspoken and not frightened to speak to people about most subjects is also part of being motivated and enthusiastic and this includes talking about my experiences of having epilepsy, bowel cancer and being unemployed. Even going for a walk or a cycle ride fills me with motivation and enthusiasm because the body is on the move and I am able to get out and about and do some exercise. Attending church services and bible studies, especially bible studies, really fills me with motivation and enthusiasm because I am studying God's word, which is really important to me and the most important thing to study. When you know that someone sacrificed their life because of your own sins and they did it so that your faith and belief in them will provide you with eternal life and perfect body it should fill you with motivation and enthusiasm big time. It does me, and it also means knowing that when Jesus Christ returns, I, like many others, will be leading a new life with a new body and eternal life. Since writing my first book I have been filled with motivation and enthusiasm because of what I am writing about and how it can help people, support people and get people interested. What I have written about may also fill my readers with motivation and enthusiasm through God's Grace because of what they have got out of it.

Having overcome epilepsy and bowel cancer has filled me with motivation and enthusiasm and every day of my life I am filled with them because having had my life saved when I was diagnosed with bowel cancer has given me a second chance in life and this was all down to God's Grace. Wherever I am and whatever situation I am in I will always be filled with motivation and enthusiasm and God knows that. As well as his Holy Spirit guiding me every day the things I am involved with fill me with motivation and enthusiasm, some more than others, but they all make me very keen to be involved in them and to do my best. The motivation and enthusiasm is internally with me and every day I can feel it and put it in to practise when going about my daily life as a Born Again Christian. I look forward to the things I am involved in all the time. Understanding and accepting the gift of God's Grace is very important to me, it certainly fills me with motivation and enthusiasm plus it never leaves me.

CHAPTER 13

Courage & Confidence

Having courage and confidence in ourselves during our lives could make a big difference in how we live our lives are. Born Again Christians are given this through God's Grace and because they understand and accept God's Grace they will find that courage and confidence will work in them throughout their lives, especially at times when they really need it. Courage and confidence are a big part of our lives and it all comes from God's free gift of his Grace. There are times in our lives when we can feel the courage and confidence working in us and not only important times but during our daily lives at any time. Born Again Christians could be in any situation and God will make sure that the courage and confidence in them is working. People who are struggling with courage and confidence and find themselves doubting themselves and feeling nervous may not realise that they are being prevented from having courage and confidence by Satan (i.e. The Devil) who wants nobody to have courage and confidence. This will more likely happen to people who are non-believers and not Born Again Christians, and have little or no faith and don't accept and understand what God's Grace is.

Making decisions, whether they are important or not, during our daily lives is a very common and regular thing, and being able have courage and confidence when putting these decisions in to practise is also important.

Born Again Christians are full of courage and confidence and most days are able to put their decisions in to practise reasonably easily and are helped by knowing that they have God's Grace in them. Non-believers and people who are not Born Again Christians, who have no faith and no understanding of God's Grace may and will find it harder to have courage and confidence when trying to make decisions during their daily lives whether they are important or not. That lack of courage and confidence could make a big difference in life. With little or no courage and confidence people are going to find it harder to put things in to practise such as: - talking to members of the general public, communication in general, interviews, cooking and housework, shopping, taking part in events and activities, speaking about health problems, overcoming problems including health problems etc.

In my own life I have needed the gifts of courage and confidence from God's Grace on many occasions. During the forty years I was affected by epilepsy which included school life, job searching, going to interviews and taking part in various activities and hobbies during my early life, I needed courage and confidence on many occasions. Being able to get over epileptic seizures and move on from them means having courage and confidence, and to speak about them and explain them as well. Quite a few people affected by epilepsy also have short term memory loss and at both school and when looking for work I had to come to terms with this plus I needed courage and confidence to cope with it and overcome it. As I got older and got closer to the time I grew out of the epilepsy it became slightly easier for me to remember things. Since I grew out of them in 2006 it has been easier for me to remember things. When I was diagnosed with bowel cancer I needed even more courage and confidence when coping with it and overcoming it. When I had many years of pain and agony with the abdominal pain and adhesions plus the twisted colon I needed much courage and confidence to know what to do to try and find a solution and to try my best to put up with what I was going through. That went on for approximately thirteen to fifteen years. Making decisions on whether I should go for a walk, go for a bike ride or play some indoor or outdoor bowls, while in pain, meant needing courage and confidence to make the right decision. If I was in too much pain, I had to give these a miss and if I was in less pain then I would push myself and give them a try. As time went by during these years it became slightly easier for me to make a decision as I was used to the situation I was in.

Having courage and confidence has also made me more outspoken and not frightened to speak about anything including various experiences I have been through during my life. Because of God's Grace, he is filling me with courage and confidence throughout my life and every day of my daily life. It is something that makes me want to be involved in things and take part in as many things as I can fit in to my life. It also helps me when attending jobcentre appointments and training courses. When I am on my bike it helps me when I need to be aware of the traffic around me and how to be careful. When I am on an outdoor bowls green courage and confidence helps me to be competitive and use as much energy as possible and to use it as part of my exercise. Being part of a walking group also fills me with courage and confidence and also helps me when exercising. Doing volunteer work and attending church services and events also fill me with courage and confidence because I am part of something and involved in something that means so much to me. The highlight of all the things I am involved in is attending a bible study each week because I am meeting a group of Born Again Christians and learning about God's Word including his Grace. This really fills me with courage and confidence and is the most important thing in my life to learn about. God is willing me to learn his word as much as possible and for me to use my courage and confidence to tell others about it because it is so important.

CHAPTER 14

Knowledge

For Born Again Christians their knowledge of God's word (the bible) grows as they study and learn about God's word (the bible), and this all comes from God's Grace because the better their knowledge of God's word (the bible) the closer they are to God. Remembering and retaining everything from the bible is not easy, some people have good memories and others not so much but the more studying and learning the better. To Born Again Christians their knowledge is important and to God it is important that Born Again Christians retain their knowledge as part of their discipleship and to magnify his word (the bible) to people who are non-believers. Although a Born Again Christian's soul and spirit is more important than their knowledge, their knowledge is still part of God's Grace and a free gift from him to study and learn his word (the bible) and by studying and learning his word (the bible) it is not only going to improve their knowledge but make life as a Born Again Christian easier. The knowledge of God's word (the bible) to a Born Again Christian makes their life easier plus if during their daily life they were to explain to a non-believer about God's word (the bible) they would also be able to give the non-believer an answer to a questions they were asked. The more knowledge, the more Born Again Christians understand about God's word (the bible). For Born Again Christians the knowledge they have of God's word (the bible) makes them feel more confident, happier, more calm and relaxed, closer to God including their friendship with him, and feel more part of God's universe. Their knowledge can also lift their spirit, know they are required as a disciple and help them to encourage others. Their knowledge can also give them the motivation and enthusiasm to tell non-believers the difference between Heaven and Hell plus the difference between being a Born Again Christian and a non-believer.

Non-believers and people who are not Born Again Christians will have little or no knowledge of God's word (the bible) and not want to either. Unfortunately for them Satan (i.e. The Devil) is working on them and trying as hard as possible to prevent them from taking any interest in God's word (the bible) and also giving them very little or no chance of gaining any knowledge. Satan (i.e. The Devil) doesn't want anyone to study or learn anything about God's word (the bible) and non-believers and people who are not Born Again Christians are letting him get his way and they have no idea that it is happening to them. Born Again Christians on the other hand know that Satan (i.e. The Devil) is not going to get his way with them because as well as God's Holy Spirit guiding them all the time and throughout their lives they know their knowledge is necessary and it is very important to them. Non-believers and people who are not Born Again Christians will have a completely different attitude and with very little or no knowledge of God's word (the bible) would not be able to give an answer if asked about God's word (the bible) by another person. This gives them a massive disadvantage during their daily lives and not wanting to be one of God's children plus not wanting to be part of his world either. Because Satan (i.e. The Devil) is taking control over non-believers and people who are not Born Again Christians he is wanting to pass on knowledge of his world instead and that is spreading bad and evil around. The only way non-believers and people who are not Born Again Christians at the present time are going to gain knowledge of God's word (the bible) is by them studying and learning plus getting help and advice from a Born Again Christian.

As a Born Again Christian, my knowledge has grown a fair bit since the mid 1980's when I first started attending house groups and bible studies. During my first 5-10 years of studying and learning I mainly had to listen to the readers and the group leaders so that I could pick things up and ask a question if and when I was given a chance to. Since the late 1990's and early 2000's I have belonged to one house group/bible study and still studying and learning with that same house group/bible study. The group leader let's each of us ask whatever questions we need to in between readings and questions. The group leader has been exceptionally helpful to me and my knowledge of God's word (the bible) has grown quite a bit through their teaching of God's word (the bible) to me. I am exceptionally grateful to them. If anyone was to ask me a question about God's word (the bible) or about my faith, belief and trust in God I would give them my honest and best answer to them. If for some reason I didn't have an answer to a question I would let them know at a later date if they were still prepared to wait for my answer and were still keen to get an answer to their question. My knowledge of God's word (the bible) is important to me as I am one of his children, he is my creator, saviour and redeemer, and my guide throughout my life, plus he has given me eternal life as well. My knowledge of God's word (the bible) also makes my life easier because as well as studying and learning it, it also makes me feel closer to him, knowing he is with me all the time plus my friendship with him is continuously on the go all the time. Through his Grace God is willing me to gain knowledge of his word (the bible) and is willing me to study and learn as much as I can. Whatever I learn from God's word (the bible) is going to of benefit to me and anyone whom I magnify God's word (the bible) to.

CHAPTER 15

<u>Hope</u>

Hope is an extremely big part of our lives and a big part of God's Grace. He wants us to have as much hope in us as we possibly can, the more the better. Being filled with hope will help us so much because we all need it and not only in bad situations but also in situations where we are looking forward to something exciting. When we are filled with hope by God's Grace and we can really feel it, it means so much to us. It is in our heart and souls all the time and it will be there whenever we need it. When we are filled with hope, accept and understand God's Grace, and are Born Again Christians, hope is in us virtually all the time and works all the time. People who don't understand or accept God's Grace, and don't want to know, will struggle to find hope and find things in life quite hard. People in this situation who haven't got hope and just make life harder for themselves and others will find that Satan (i.e. The Devil) will be doing his best to give them no hope and make them feel depressed and keep giving up on things. Throughout their lives they will be going through hard times and not having that hope inside them due to very little or no understanding of God's Grace will only make things even harder still. Very little or no hope in a person will make things such as problems with health, finances, personal, employment and many others harder still for that person. People who live in a competitive world, people who are involved in sports and games that include trying to win will also life hard if they can't accept not winning and give up early on. It means the hope they have is very little or none at all. Some people who have very negative ways during their daily lives will also find that they will have very little or no hope because of how they are thinking and feeling at the time. These hopeless thoughts and feelings are all due to Satan (i.e. The Devil) because he wants the worst for everyone.

   During my life I have been filled with hope due to God's Grace, especially since 2000 when I was diagnosed with bowel cancer and survived it. When I go about my daily life I can actually feel the hope in me and I never give up on any situations, even when there is a slight problem. Having suffered between 13 and 15 years of abdominal pain and adhesions plus a twisted colon, and being able to not worry at all, filled me with a huge amount of hope, and that has stayed with me and will never leave me. The hope in me as part of the gift of God's Grace is sky high and that is what he wants me to have. It is so wonderful to be able to be filled with hope. It certainly does help. I have been in many situations where the hope in me has been necessary and been put in to practise. I had many years of epilepsy and although I had forty years of it I always stayed hopeful and eventually grew out of it when I was forty-four years old. From 1978, at the age of sixteen, I have been job searching and most years I have been looking for work for either a few months or the whole of the year. With the amount of hope in me it has kept me going to this very day. Since 1980 I have been involved in both indoor and outdoor bowls, and on many occasions I have won and on many occasions

I have lost games. I have also drawn several as well. Whenever I have lost it has never put me off due to all the hope inside me. I am hoping to carry on participating in this sport as long as I possibly can. Since I was sixteen years-old I have also been cycling, not as a sport, as a hobby and using a traditional bicycle but even though I am getting slightly slower now I will carry on cycling for as long as I possibly can because the hope inside me keeps me going.

When we are filled with hope as part of God's Grace it not only helps us in our own daily lives but it can also help us to try and help and support others who don't possess much or any hope in them. Whenever I hear people talking in either a negative way or speaking as if they are going to give up on a particular thing or situation in their life I try and give them hope as much as I possibly can. I try and think of solutions and go through it with them and try and give them hope by trying to let them know that giving up on something or a situation will not help them in any way at all. Being hopeful, trying to make progress and trying to make the best of a bad thing or situation will eventually work, especially if they try their hardest to put it into practise. If someone is finding something really hard in life but they stay hopeful things will gradually improve and as long as the hope continues to be there in them and doesn't fade or disappear. Satan (i.e. The Devil) will try his hardest to make the hope disappear in people but they must not let him. I have been in many situations and the hope in me has made me progress and overcome quite a few things. Satan (i.e. The Devil) will try his hardest to make the hope in me disappear but it won't because of God's Grace in me. When someone is a Born Again Christian God's Grace in them will never disappear.

CHAPTER 16

Faith, Belief & Trust

Having faith, belief and trust in our Lord is a huge part of our daily lives. Those who are Born Again Christians will have more understanding of faith, belief and trust than those who are not. Our Lord not only wants us to have faith, belief and trust in him but he also provides us with faith, belief and trust as part of his Grace. A Born Again Christian's soul will be filled with faith, belief and trust for our Lord. It is so important for us to have faith, belief and trust in God because we are not only closer to him but we understand what he has provided us with and he wants everything good for us to happen to us. Some people's faith, belief and trust in God is exceptionally strong and some people's not quite so strong. How we feel about God and our understanding of his Grace is very important because the more we understand the more likely we are to have more faith, belief and trust in him. How we live our daily lives and how we deal with things, even when we are going through hard times, can make a big difference. Having faith, belief and trust in God also means when we are experiencing problems and going through hard times we don't blame him for them because we know that God is blameless because he is perfect. With a strong understanding of faith, belief and trust in God and feeling it we are also more likely to praise him when we are experiencing good times in our lives.

People who are not Born Again Christians are less likely to understand and accept faith, belief and trust in God through his Grace, they may not even want to have anything to do with faith, belief and trust in God. Unfortunately, Satan (i.e. The Devil) will be doing his best to prevent people from having faith, belief and trust in God, and trying to get them to turn away from God altogether. Satan (i.e. The Devil) will also be trying his hardest to remove any faith, belief and trust in God people have and trying his hardest to make them blame God for all their problems. People who blame God for their problems or for anything else unfortunately don't realise that God is blameless and is perfect. With no feelings at all for God there are going to be people whose faith, belief and trust in him is just non-existent. With no faith, belief and trust in God people will find life much harder and also no understanding of praising him when they need to. There are also many other religions who think they have faith, belief and trust in God but if they are not Born Again Christians their idea of faith, belief and trust in God will be all for nothing and that is the work of Satan (i.e. The Devil) leading them in the wrong direction.

During my life, the life I have lead so far and the experiences I have had so far have drawn me closer to God as time has moved on and it has also made my faith, belief and trust in him extremely strong. When I was diagnosed with bowel cancer, when I experienced abdominal pain and adhesions and when I experienced a twisted colon it certainly made my faith, belief and trust in God extremely strong. The moment I was told I had my life saved I was not only extremely surprised but also knew that God had given me another chance to carry on living my life on earth. The feeling of having my life saved also made me feel through faith, belief and trust in God, exceptional thankful and grateful. Our Lord knows who has faith, belief and trust in him and who doesn't. God knew I had faith, belief and trust in him well before I was ever diagnosed with bowel cancer and through that I had my life saved. He also knew it before I was even born. Even when I have experienced other problems and hard times including when I had forty years of epilepsy and when I had many years of unemployment I have always kept my faith, belief and trust in God to help me overcome them and be able to cope with them. I also know that as I go through my daily life my faith, belief and trust in God is going to make my life easier. Our Lord doesn't want anyone to suffer, come to any harm or for anything bad to happen to anyone, and that includes me. Saying prayers and even talking to my Lord during my daily life makes me feel as if my faith, belief and trust in him is there and I am closer to him. My faith, belief and trust in God also gives me more positivity and puts that feeling in to me during my daily life, it also helps me when talking to people who are not so positive. Having faith, belief and trust in God not only makes a lot of difference in a human's life but it can also make a big difference in how they behave, react and communicate with others. The closeness of God inside a human is wonderful and is a great feeling because having God there with us all the time, wherever we maybe, is a massive boost to us. I can feel him in me all the time because he is guiding me and I know he wants the best for me during my life. My faith, belief and trust in God means I know that whenever anything bad happens or goes wrong in my life I know to blame Satan (i.e. The Devil) and not God. I know that God is blameless at all times, and is perfect. Although I have hard times like many others I have also had a lot of luck but most of that may have been through my faith, belief and trust in God.

CHAPTER 17
Being Saved & Salvation

Being saved and salvation is also an exceptionally important part of our lives, especially for Born Again Christians. When we receive and accept God's Grace it is a massive gift from him and as part of it Born Again Christians will be saved. Understanding that Jesus Christ died for us on the cross (the resurrection) because of all the sins we each commit and that he was raised from the dead by God the Father plus having faith, belief and trust in him is for Born Again Christians being saved and salvation. For Born Again Christians being saved and salvation is in their minds and is part of their daily lives. How we behave, react, communicate and go about our daily lives will also have an effect on us knowing we are being saved. Understanding what being saved and salvation is can also makes us think differently and how we go about our daily lives in a way where we know each day we have our Lord with us all the time and he is willing us to have faith, belief and trust in him for our own benefits. For Born Again Christians it is also easier to explain to other people what being saved and salvation means and why we are saved. The difference between a person being saved and a person not being saved is massive and is the most important thing in the world to those who believe in being saved and salvation. Through Jesus Christ dying on the cross (the resurrection) and God raising him from dead, God the Father wants us to be saved and be with him in Heaven. The day Jesus Christ returns those of us that are Born Again Christians and have been saved will go with him to Heaven. This will not only happen suddenly but a person who has been saved could be next to a person who has not been saved, one will go with Jesus Christ to Heaven and one will not.

Satan (i.e. The Devil) is hoping that we are not saved by trying his hardest to persuade us to reject and not receive God's Grace and not understand it either. People who have no faith, belief and trust in God and have no intention of doing so at any time in their lives will not be saved. Having no understanding and no idea of what being saved and salvation is and no thought of finding out either will end up being a massive mistake in anyone's lives. Because of what Satan (i.e. The Devil) is trying to do to us all and with some people, even quite a large number of people, he is succeeding, he will be preventing people from being saved and from going to Heaven with our Lord as well. Anyone who is not saved will end up going to Hell along with Satan (i.e. The Devil). We are either saved or not saved, no other alternatives. It is the same as going to Heaven or Hell, with no other alternatives. People who are not Born Again Christians will also find out because of how they behave, react, communicate and go about their daily lives will also have an effect on them not being saved. Some people struggle to believe in our Lord and sometimes blame God for their problems instead of Satan (i.e. The Devil), this will prevent them from being saved. Not believing that Jesus Christ died on the cross (the resurrection) because of our sins and God raising him from dead will also prevent people from being saved and will also be a huge mistake in anyone's life. Quite a few things as well as a lack of or no faith, belief and trust in God can prevent people from being saved including being weak, negative and pessimistic, disorganised, bad behaviour, unloving and many other things. Being undecided about believing and being saved plus salvation is just as bad for anyone because there are only two alternatives. People are either for or against, nothing else. The return of Jesus Christ could happen at any time.

Throughout my life so far, especially since I started going to church in the 1980's and attending bible studies, my knowledge and understanding of the bible (God's word/scripture) has grown and got stronger and stronger. Understanding that Jesus Christ died on the cross (the resurrection) because of my sins and God raising him from dead has become so important to me. I think about it quite often during my daily life, more so now than I did years ago. Being a Born Again Christian is really important to me as is being saved and salvation, which is the most important thing in the world to me. Being a Born Again Christian and being saved to me helps me so much in my daily life. How I think, behave, react, communicate, pray and many other things included and are all positive. Being saved and salvation is also exceptionally important to me because of knowing that it means not only being in Heaven with our Lord but it also means having a new body, no suffering ever again and a completely new life. Through being saved and salvation my life in Heaven is going to be massively different to the life I have been living and am still living at the present time. Being saved and salvation also helps me know that when I sin, it helps me to repent from these sins as soon as possible plus say a pray for saying sorry and asking for forgiveness. Knowing that I am a Born Again Christian and saved also helps me when dealing with and overcoming problems and hard times. The feeling of being saved and salvation, having a new body and living a pain free life is inside me nearly all the time. It is something I am looking forward to and it gives me such a positive and exciting feeling inside me. For me, meeting Jesus Christ is going to be such a big thing, knowing that he sacrificed his life on the cross, and because he wanted to give me a chance of living a perfect life. The only reason I have been sinning is because of Satan (i.e. The Devil) being in this world at the present time.

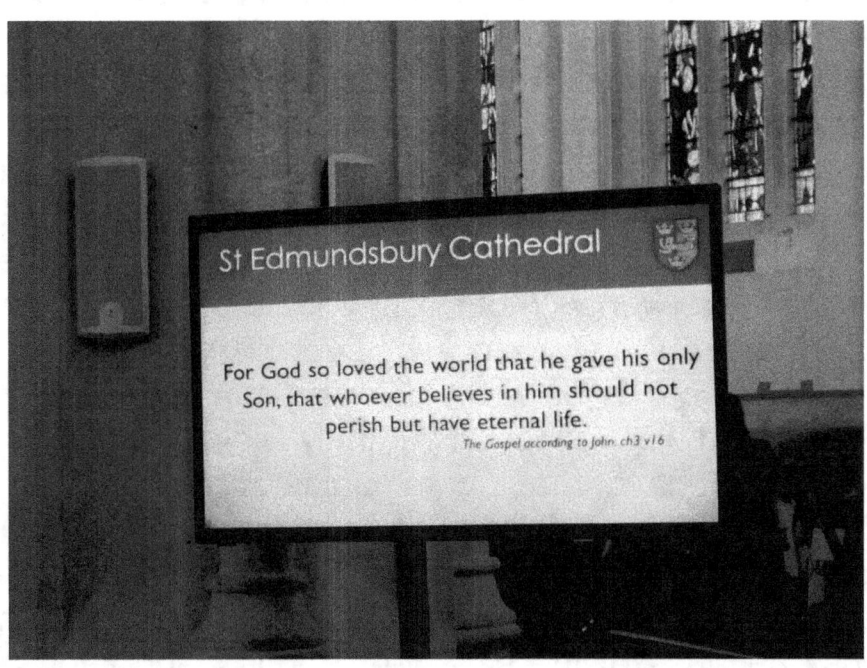

CHAPTER 18

Eternal Life

Eternal life is not only part of our lives now if we are Born Again Christians and have faith, belief and trust in God but once we are in Heaven life will be eternal for the rest of our new lives with our Lord and Saviour. Eternal life is also part of God's Grace that we receive as a free gift from him. If we want eternal life to be part of our lives believing in our Lord is exceptionally important and is an essential part of our daily lives. Knowing that our bodies and lives will be completely perfect when we are in Heaven with our Lord should be in our minds throughout our daily lives, whatever we may be doing, wherever we may be and whatever situation we are in. That should also reflect on our daily lives including how we think, behave, react, communicate, pray and many other things. Eternal life in Heaven is going to be that good, there is nothing else better we could wish for, and this is all due to Jesus Christ sacrificing his life on the cross because of the sins we commit. God knows a Born Again Christian and a person who understands about sin and true repentance during their daily lives. The feeling of eternal life, even before the return of Jesus Christ has taken place, is to a lot of people both quite rewarding but also the best thing we have to look forward to. Sometimes we can imagine what eternal life in Heaven is going to be like but in reality we have very little chance of knowing until the return of our Saviour

Jesus Christ. There are a few details that maybe known and they are things such as; a new body, a new life, no suffering and pain ever again, no need for money ever again, no need for time (clocks/watches etc.), complete light and a perfect life. Having eternal life before the return of our Saviour Jesus Christ is something that Born Again Christians are not only aware of but receive as a gift as part of God's Grace.

People that are non-believers and not Born Again Christians will not believe in God and the return of Jesus Christ, and have no intentions of doing so will not have eternal life and instead of it being in Heaven it will be in Hell. For people who are not Born Again Christians and never intend to be eternal life in Hell will be exceptionally hard. This is all down to Satan (i.e. The Devil) and his plans to prevent people from being Born Again Christians. These are people that commit sins and have no intentions of saying sorry or repenting from them. Most of them have no understanding of what their punishment is going to be because of not being a Born Again Christian. Eternal life in Hell is going to be that bad it can't get any worse and it is going to be much worse than the life people are living at the present time. This will also apply to people who are undecided about believing in God and the return of Jesus Christ, and have no intentions of changing their minds. Eternal life will be in one of two places only; those who are Born Again Christians will be in Heaven with God and those who are not Born Again Christians will be in Hell with Satan (i.e. The Devil), there is nowhere else. Being undecided is just as bad as saying no for definite because the return of Jesus Christ could happen any time and when it does it will happen very suddenly as well. If people are currently undecided and want eternal life to be in Heaven rather than Hell they need to start believing in God, studying his word (scripture/the bible), start understanding about sin and repenting. They also need to realise that the differences between eternal life in Heaven and eternal life in Hell are massive, and for the rest of their lives, once we have had the return of our Saviour Jesus Christ. For quite a few people having a lack of or no faith, belief and trust in God, having no understanding of scripture/the bible or always blaming God for their problems will prevent them from becoming Born Again Christians and will make it harder for them to understand that they could and possibly will end up living eternal life in Hell rather than Heaven. If they want to be living eternal life now and in Heaven they need to start believing in God, studying his word (scripture/the bible), start understanding about sin and repenting etc. How they live their daily lives is also important especially if they want to become a Born Again Christian.

During the years I have been a Born Again Christian and regularly attending church services and bible studies my knowledge of eternal life has grown and got stronger and stronger. Other Born Again Christians who I see on a regular basis discuss eternal life in Heaven from time to time and although discussing it isn't easy we sometimes talk about the few things that are known to us and even quite a few things we have no idea of. The majority of things about eternal life in Heaven are unknown to most people and can only be imagined. Being saved and speaking about eternal life on earth is easier because it is the present and the future before the return of Jesus

Christ. Having been given God's Grace this gift is also providing us with eternal life because God wants us to not only believe in him, have the best things in life before the return of our Saviour Jesus Christ but also to be with him when we are in Heaven. What we receive from God is the best we can ever receive.

CHAPTER 19

Justice

God's justice is certainly important and as part of his Grace we need to realise that it is as essential as the rest of his Grace. For Born Again Christians, when we commit sins we know about it and we say sorry to God and mean it 100% plus ask for forgiveness and repent from the sins by putting it into practice. Throughout their daily lives they commit sins and as well as the bad deeds and words they also need to repent from bad thoughts as well. Some sins they don't notice but the majority of the time Born Again Christians do know when they have committed a sin and should know how to say sorry to God, ask for forgiveness and repent from their sins. God knows when Born Again Christians are genuine and say sorry to him, ask for forgiveness and repent from their sins. The day Jesus Christ returns and Born Again Christians go with him to Heaven, and because of God's justice they will all be judged not guilty. The majority of Born Again Christians will be aware of their sins during their daily lives and will repent from them on a regular basis including saying prayers to our Lord. Knowing what sins are, accepting that you have sinned, knowing how to ask for forgiveness and repent from sins plus being a genuine and true Born Again Christian has a massive advantage. Born Again Christians have God with them every day of their lives, wherever they maybe, and he will know when they sin. Knowing this is also a massive advantage to Born Again Christians because in their minds they know they need to try and control their thoughts, words and actions throughout their daily lives and what to do when they have sinned.

For people who are not Born Again Christians, understanding God's justice will not be so easy and for most will be virtually impossible. For those who have little or no faith, belief and trust in God and have no intentions of doing so, if Jesus Christ were to return and they were still non-believers, they would be judged guilty and be on their way to Hell along with Satan (i.e. The Devil). A good majority of people who are not Born Again Christians will commit sins and have no idea of what they have been doing plus have no idea that God is watching them during their daily lives as well. Most know that they are doing wrong but don't realise they are committing sins and have no thought at all of repenting from them. Satan (i.e. The Devil) is unfortunately doing his best to make people commit as many sins as possible and do as much bad as they can. He is also trying to prevent people from understanding what God's justice is. Some people, throughout their daily lives, are just intending to have bad thoughts, say bad words and do bad deeds, with no thought of the outcome and other people's feelings and lives. If people continue in that way throughout their lives it will get harder for them to repent from their sins and harder for them to understand what God's justice is. A good majority of people who continue to intentionally sin without repentance not only have very little understanding of God's justice but also deny that it is even true. In that situation they are letting the power of Satan (i.e. The Devil) get to them and take over their lives. That includes people of other religions, non-believers and people who are involved in LGBTQ. For people who deny the truth including that they sin and want to ignore God's justice the fact is that when Jesus Christ returns they will be on their way to Hell a long with Satan (i.e. The Devil). The quality of life in Hell, even though the exact details are unknown, will be much worse than on earth.

Throughout my life, through all the ups and downs I have had, my understanding of God's justice has got stronger and stronger, and this is also due to God's Grace being with me all the time. As time has gone on my understanding of what sinning is has got stronger and stronger and so I recognise my sins and not only say sorry for them but also ask for forgiveness as well. I also put it in to practise to repent from these sins and try my hardest to not do them again. There are times when I haven't realised when I have sinned but most of the time I do. Some of the sins I have committed, I say prayers for as soon as it has happened. Others, I say prayers for at the end of the day. This could include any bad thoughts I had or bad words I said and didn't notice. Sometimes this may happen if during my daily life I am extra busy and the mind and body are quite active. Being a Born Again Christian I don't doubt in my Lord, and I know and have faith, belief and trust in him to show the power of his justice towards me, as part of his Grace, especially when my Saviour Jesus Christ returns. The fact that I am a Born Again Christian and I understand God's justice makes me live my life in a more calm and relaxed way even though life isn't always easy. The fact that God's justice is part of his Grace makes it easier for me as a Born Again Christian to live my daily life and know that God's justice really does work. I am aware of my sins a good majority of the time during my daily life and I know that God wants me to obey him by saying sorry, ask for forgiveness and repent from the sins that I have committed. When I repent from my sins God's justice comes in to action and he forgives me. As I am a Born Again Christian and because I know God's justice works it helps me to sin less often.

CHAPTER 20
Righteousness & Holiness

For Born Again Christians to be filled with righteousness and holiness through God's Grace it is a massive thing and a wonderful thing as well. As Born Again Christians, we are filled with righteousness and holiness because God's wants us to have faith, belief and trust in him forever. The closer we are to him and the stronger our understanding of him the better. As Born Again Christians, the better our understanding of our Saviour Jesus Christ's birth and resurrection the better it is for us. During our daily lives we are filled with righteousness and holiness, and that should help us in how we go about how we behave, think, talk, react and deal with things in general. Living a Christian life including recognising our sins and repenting from them is all part of us being filled will righteousness and holiness. Everything God wants for us is his gift of his Grace and we need to be thankful and grateful for that, and obey his word (scripture/bible) during our eternal life on earth. Being filled with righteousness and holiness to Born Again Christians means a lot because we are aware of his presence throughout our lives and it is very important. The more of us that are filled with righteousness and holiness, the better it is. Being filled with righteousness and holiness can also make us closer to God and our relationship and friendship with him as well. God is also guiding us through our daily lives through his Holy Spirit as well. God will also know who is obeying him and who has righteousness and holiness. We can talk and pray to God at any time and the more righteousness and holiness we have in us the easier it is for us to do this. For Born Again Christians to be filled with righteousness and holiness is also a wonderful feeling because you are not only living eternal life on earth but it gives you a wonderful feeling that you are following and obeying God's word (scripture/bible). Being filled with righteousness and holiness has a massive and the biggest ever reward a person could have and that is a place in Heaven with our Saviour Jesus Christ.

For people who are not Born Again Christians and no intensions of being so, righteousness and holiness will be impossible. Satan (i.e. The Devil) will trying his hardest to prevent as many people as possible to be filled with righteousness and holiness because he wants them to sin as much as possible and turn away from God. He wants them to ignore and disobey God's word (scripture/bible) as much as they can as well. Not being filled with righteousness and holiness will make life so much harder. Ignoring and disobeying God's word (scripture/bible) will also have an effect on how people think, behave, react and communicate and for most people righteousness and holiness won't exist due to Satan (i.e. The Devil). In fact, he will make them more unrighteous and unholy as time goes by. Unfortunately, there are many people whose lack of understanding what righteousness and holiness is and what it means, who will suffer in various ways during both their earthly lives and beyond. Some people who are filled with hatred, continually sinning without repenting and carry on in life with no care or love for others will really struggle to be filled with righteousness and holiness. Not being filled with righteousness and holiness means people will have the worst outcome in life as possible and that is a place in Hell a long with Satan (i.e. The Devil). That will be eternal as well. Because of what Satan (i.e. The Devil) is doing to people in the world, their feelings for him are stronger and stronger, and that means their feelings for God don't exist. People can also be unrighteous and unholy due to believing in other religions other than Christianity because none of them are to do with God's word (scripture/bible). Studying religions other than Christianity will help nobody and will leave them further away from God than ever.

Being filled with God's Grace has not only helped me throughout my life but it has also filled me with righteousness and holiness. I have been through many ups and downs, some very testing, some very scary and some very exciting. Through attending church services and bible studies, as well as being with God every day of my daily life, my righteousness and holiness has got stronger and stronger. My thoughts and feelings for my Lord are with him every day and I also ask him to be with me and stay with me wherever I maybe and in whatever situation I am in, this includes guiding me every day and being able to overcome and cope with hard times in my life. Throughout my life my Lord has been getting closer to me and I can actually feel him holding on to me when he is guiding me throughout my daily life. I could be indoors at home, outdoors on my bike, doing volunteer work, shopping, on the outdoor bowls green, at the Jobcentre, in church or anywhere else, but whichever one it is God's righteousness and holiness is still in me. The stronger my faith is and the closer to God I am, the longer the righteousness and holiness will be in me. I have faith in God to keep guiding me throughout the whole of my life on earth and fill me with righteousness and holiness for the rest of my life. Talking to other Born Again Christians at regular bible studies really does help me a lot and being close to those people also helps me. Discussing God's word (scripture/bible) with others is a wonderful thing as is learning from others. Studying God's word (scripture/bible) and the righteousness and holiness in me helps me so much more. Being filled with righteousness and holiness also makes me want to study God's word (scripture/bible) even more and makes me very keen to find out and learn as much as I possibly can. As a matter of fact, there is no limit to how much I can find out and learn about God's word (scripture/bible) because I can keep learning forever and ever. I am very thankful and grateful to be filled with righteousness and holiness and all because of God's Grace.

CHAPTER 21

Fearlessness

Because we receive God's Grace continuously when we are Born Again Christians we are also filled with fearlessness and that helps us throughout our daily lives to not worry or be frightened of things or people. One of the chapter titles in scripture/the bible is "Do Not Worry" and that is in Luke chapter 12, verses 22-34. Being filled with fearlessness will also help us in how we think, behave, react and communicate each day of our lives. We all go through good and bad times and through the bad or hard times being filled with fearlessness will make us stronger and believe in ourselves. Believing in ourselves plus being filled with fearlessness will also help us to make light work of a problem and a minimum amount of fuss about a problem as well. It will help us when it comes to helping us search for a solution and putting it in to practise until it works. It means we are determined to resolve our problems and overcome the bad and hard times we have. God is also determined to help us overcome our problems plus will try and prevent us having those problems we have in the first place. His Grace is that big and important. The fearlessness in us will also make us more outgoing and more likely to join in things, speak out, help people and be more active. Sometimes the fearlessness in us means when we have a problem we are either able to put up with it for as long as need be or we are able to resolve it fairly easily.

The fearlessness in us also increases the positivity in us plus increases our faith in God as well.

People who are not Born Again Christians and have no intentions of being so will find fearlessness is either not in them or their idea of fearlessness is completely different and wrong. People of other religions or of no religion at all may not be frightened or fearful of things or people during their lives but their understanding of God plus his Grace being with them is just non-existent. Because Satan (i.e. The Devil) is trying to invade their lives he is going to get to people who are not Born Again Christians and will try and cause as many problems as possible, and that will eventually make the fearfulness in them disappear. That means people will end up being more fearful because their lack of understanding and accepting God's Grace will really let them down. That also includes their lack of understanding and accepting God's word (scripture/the bible). People who think they are fearless about things that happen during their daily lives including going through bad and hard times will struggle because they have little or no faith in God at all. Satan (i.e. The Devil) will also be working on people and be trying to put fear in to them and make them worried, scared, anxious etc. This could affect people in all situations during their lives. Negativity and pessimism will also affect people during their lives and instead of thinking and being determined to resolve a problem it will make people do nothing and let the problem gradually get worse. With no faith in God people who are not Born Again Christians will find the fear in them will gradually grow without them realising it and that is something they don't need.

As a Born Again Christian, both my experiences I have been through and my strong faith in God has filled me with fearlessness, and that helps me in my daily life a lot. When I had my experiences of epilepsy and bowel cancer being filled with fearlessness helped me so much and this was all down to me receiving and accepting God's Grace throughout my daily life. God's Grace is the most special thing in the world I can receive and it means so much including being filled with fearlessness. Because the fearlessness in me is working it makes my daily life easier even if I do have hard or bad times. I make myself find a solution or resolve my problems with no fuss. It also helps me help others with very little or no fuss when it comes to resolving their problems. Being filled with fearlessness helps me when talking and communicating with people. It also helps me along with other reasons to speak to people about my faith and why I am a Born Again Christian. Being filled with fearlessness also makes me feel as if I have more freedom and am able to going about things without being worried, scared, anxious etc. Knowing that God is with me all the time is also a big factor in my life, he fills me with fearlessness and helps me when praying and talking to him. This happens on a daily basis. The more fearlessness God fills me with the better, because it means my daily life is going to be made easier and it will also make me realise that God is with me and following me everywhere I go and is with me forever. The feeling of fearlessness is like the feeling of safety or security. When I was going through the experiences of abdominal pain, adhesions and a twisted colon, after I was diagnosed with bowel cancer God filled me with extreme fearlessness and that prevented me becoming mentally or emotionally affected. Because of the fearlessness inside me I knew that worrying would have done no good and that staying calm and relaxed would help me even though I had to put up with a lot of physical pain and agony. The fearlessness stayed with me throughout all the years I went through this experience. Whatever situation I am in during my daily life God's presence is with me and he knows that because he is with me I am going to be able to cope in one way or another. He knows I will try my hardest to find a solution and resolve it as soon as possible.

CHAPTER 22

Mercy

For Born Again Christians God's mercy is with them and works in them throughout their daily lives if they accept and understand his Grace. The closer we are to God and the stronger our faith in him is, his mercy will be working in us. We need God's mercy all the time, whatever situation we are in. Receiving God's mercy in our lives can make a big difference in how we talk, behave and communicate with other people. Born Again Christians still sin during their lives but in receiving God's mercy they will know how to ask for forgiveness and repent from those sins, plus make sure it doesn't happen again. It isn't easy because all humans sin, even a bad thought which is not recognised, and gets forgotten about. Born Again Christians know that God's mercy will help and guide them to try and not sin in the first place plus also recognise their sins and repent from them. In knowing that they have sinned, asked for forgiveness and repented from a sin or sins he will forgive them as part of his mercy. Receiving God's mercy is also receiving his love and kindness and it not only helps them in their daily lives but it will show in their character throughout their lives. The mercy they receive from God will also help them to show mercy towards other people. Getting the feeling of God's mercy throughout their lives will certainly help them. There are many forms of mercy they receive from God and there are also many ways they can show mercy towards other people. When Born Again Christians are experiencing pain and going through hard times God's mercy shows in them when we pray for it. He doesn't want them to be in pain or suffer and never will do. God shows his mercy all the time but whether they accept it or not is up to them. The fact that Jesus Christ died upon the cross for all the sins they commit during their lives is part of God's mercy.

People who are not Born Again Christians and have no intentions of being so, plus have no intentions of believing in our Lord, will not be shown mercy by God and will find it harder to accept it or understand it. Because God is not showing his mercy towards non-believers receiving it is impossible even if they are going through hard times and struggling. They will also find it harder to overcome these problems because of their lack of or having no faith in our Lord. They need to accept God's mercy in their lives, if not life may get harder still. Satan (i.e. The Devil) will be trying his hardest to prevent them being shown mercy by God and will be trying his hardest to make them have no mercy towards other people in their lives. It will make things seriously hard and with very little or no mercy life won't be easy. Satan (i.e. The Devil) himself has no mercy towards anyone in this universe, in fact he has the least amount of mercy of anyone in the world. Because he has no mercy at all he wants us to have as many problems as possible during our lives including having as many illnesses and financial problems as we can. There is nobody worse than Satan (i.e. The Devil). Some people who have very little or no thought of how they speak, behave, communicate or react to other people will be showing very little or no mercy.

In my personal life my Lord has been showing me mercy in all different situations of my life and is still doing so. He is not only with me and showing me mercy throughout my daily life but he has been with me whenever I have sinned and he knew when I realised my sins and I asked for forgiveness and repented from those sins. As a Born Again Christian I am also likely to recognise my sins, ask for forgiveness and repent from them in the future as well. This is also part of God's mercy being with me. With all the hard and testing times I have been through during my life and through God's mercy being with all those who have helped and supported me throughout those times he has shown me mercy throughout my healing. His mercy also gave me and still gives me strength and determination. These included the years I was affected by epilepsy, bowel cancer and unemployment. Every day God's mercy is with me and it helps me in various ways including how I speak, behave, react and communicate towards people. Having God's mercy also keeps me so positive, whatever happens in my life. God's mercy is also inside me and follows me wherever I go even when I am studying his word, saying prayers and talking to him. Knowing that I am receiving God's mercy is a wonderful thing because it is a massive thing to me and to have it throughout my daily life is so important. God's mercy also lasts forever and ever. The strength of God's mercy is exceptionally strong and it will be there and work in those of us, like myself, when we accept it, understand it and let it be with us all the time. When I have shown mercy to others throughout my life, whatever it maybe, that is through God's mercy being with me. The good thoughts, words and deeds I perform during my life are part of God's mercy being with me and the longer that happens the better. God's mercy being with me all the time throughout my daily life also gives me a strong feeling of freedom and being able to go through life without worrying, panicking or being scared of anything. It also keeps me calm, relaxed and helps me think of that if a problem exists I will be able to find a solution in one way or another.

CHAPTER 23

Born Again

For people who are true Christians and have true and genuine faith, belief and trust in Jesus Christ, and continue to do so for the rest of their earthly lives they are Born Again Christians. As well as studying God's word in scripture/the bible and behaving like a Born Again Christian throughout their lives and going along with God's word they will be saved. Recognising their sins, asking for forgiveness and repenting from their sins should be easier for a Born Again Christian. Conducting themselves, how they behave, speak, communicate and react to others should also be a lot easier to Born Again Christians because they know in their heart and souls not to sin and what a sin is, this includes any bad thoughts, words and deeds. The benefit of being a Born Again Christian during your earthly life is massive. Having a life in Heaven with our Lord to look forward to is a massive thing and the biggest and best thing in anyone's life. Nothing can better that. Being Born Again is not only massive but understanding that God created the world we live in throughout our lives and that his son Jesus Christ died on the cross for all of our sins, and his Holy Spirit is guiding us throughout our earthly lives. Being a Born Again Christian also comes from being filled with God's Grace. Being a Born Again Christian during your earthly life makes you feel so much different when you go about your daily life because you have the thoughts and feelings of Jesus Christ returning and what you have to look forward to when he does return. Born Again Christians also know and believe that Jesus Christ died for all the sins mankind commits because of God's love for all of us. When Born Again Christians say prayers and they don't get instant answers to them they persist in saying them and keep patient until it is answered, even if it takes years to be answered.

For people who are not Christians including other religions, and have no intentions of being so, and for people who are Christians in their minds but not in reality then being Born Again is not likely unless they change and happen to convert. Not understanding scripture/the bible and having no intentions of doing so will be very hard or even impossible for some people. Satan (i.e. The Devil) will be trying his very hardest as he always does to prevent people from being Born Again because he wants as many people as possible to join him in Hell. For people who are not Born Again their earthly life will not only be harder than a Born Again Christian but most don't understand that living their lives in Hell will be the worst thing ever. Once they are in Hell there is no going back. The negative and bad behaviour, attitude, communication and reactions of people who are not Born Again can be a big problem and they are all down to Satan (i.e. The Devil), the longer things stay that way the harder it will be for someone to change and convert. People who are not Born Again because of little or no belief and faith in our Lord sometimes think are is another place to go and think there is no such place as Hell. Unfortunately, when Jesus Christ returns, there will be no other choice for people who are not Born

Again because the only place for them will be Hell.

My personal experience as a Born Again Christian has grown and grown as I have aged during my life. My regular understanding of scripture/the bible has just grown and grown as time has gone by and it has made me feel closer and closer to God as time has gone by. It hasn't been easy and when I first became a Christian studying wasn't quite so easy. During my daily life on earth and in everything I am involved in being a Born Again Christian makes me feel so different because I know what I have to look forward to when my Saviour Jesus Christ returns. A place and a life in Heaven is going to be so much different to the life I am currently living on earth. Because I am a Born Again Christian, understanding and knowing when I have sinned and when to ask for forgiveness and repent from sins, life becomes easier and I know that I have to put it in to action as well. Saying prayers as a Born Again Christian is also important to me. Being a Born Again Christian has also filled me with a lot of positivity and optimism because of the experiences I have been through and managed to overcome plus what I have got to look forward to when I am in Heaven with our Lord. I also know that during my daily life on earth God's Holy Spirit is guiding me in the right direction and God the Father is talking to me as well. Because I know he wants the best for me I want him to be in control of my life. It is a wonderful feeling to have during your life. God also knows that the strength, determination, positivity and optimism he has filled me with will be working in me throughout the rest of my earthly life. What God does for me to make my life as good as he wants me to have is beyond any limit. There is no limit to what good God can do for me any anyone else in this universe. Being a Born Again Christian means so much to me because it is the best thing in the world that could have ever happened to me. It all comes down to me receiving God's Grace and accepting and understanding it.

CHAPTER 24
Forgiveness & Repentance

Forgiveness and repentance are certainly important in our lives, virtually every day of our lives. Without God's Grace we wouldn't understand it or be able to put forgiveness and repentance in to practise. Born Again Christians know when they have sinned and know that by asking for forgiveness and repenting as soon as possible, the better things will be. That can be done wherever they maybe and in whatever situation they maybe in. Asking for forgiveness and repenting after committing a sin certainly has to be put in to practise because we won't receive God's forgiveness. The stronger our faith and the closer we are to God the easier it should be. When Born Again Christians recognise their sins they also know that the reason they committed them was because of Satan (i.e. The Devil). God's Grace is not only with us throughout our daily lives but he provides us with this free gift to try and prevent us sinning in the first place. God's Grace is so important because he doesn't want us to have to ask for forgiveness and repent but due to the presence of Satan (i.e. The Devil) we do. There are so many reasons and in many situations where we need to ask for forgiveness and repent. From the biggest sins to the very smallest sins, they are all as bad as one another because they shouldn't exist at any time. Bad thoughts, words and deeds all count as sins. The more we can avoid sinning the less we need to ask for forgiveness and repent. Asking for forgiveness and repenting every day during our lives is a good thing because we are more likely to have forgotten some of the sins we committed or not even realised we have sinned and we have. This also applies to Born Again Christians.

For people who are not Born Again Christians and have no intentions of being so, recognising sins and knowing what they are will have no meaning to them because of both lack of or no understanding of God's Grace plus Satan (i.e. The Devil) invading their lives. For people who sin on a regular basis and don't realise this and don't care about it, life could get much harder for them. Some people have very little feeling or knowledge of what sinning is and they think they have no need to ask for forgiveness and repent. Satan (i.e. The Devil) will not only try his hardest to make people sin as much as they can but he will also try and make them think there is no need to ask for forgiveness and repent and to just carry on sinning forever. People who don't know they are sinning and have the idea that it doesn't matter, and it means nothing to them, will find out they are making a massive mistake. There are some people who don't realise that the smallest of sins like a bad thought count as a sin, and that it happens nearly every day of their lives. Not being able to ask for forgiveness and repent during people's daily lives will make life not only harder but not recognising sins will make the way people behave, react and communicate very tricky. Without realising what sin is and forgiveness and repenting, people who are not Born Again Christians are limiting their chances of going to Heaven with our Lord and that is all due to Satan (i.e. The Devil). People who are not Born Again Christians need to learn what sin is and what forgiveness and repenting are, and try and recognise during their daily lives when they sinning. They also need to know they need to say sorry plus practise on asking for forgiveness and repent from those sins they have committed. The sooner they start practising this, the better. Because Satan (i.e. The Devil) is trying to take control of their lives as much as he possibly can people who are not Born Again Christians are going to find it harder to accept they are sinning and that asking for forgiveness and repenting are just not necessary. Born Again Christians need to help those who are not and the best thing for them is praying to our Lord on behalf of those who have no faith at the present time.

Since I first started attending church and became a Born Again Christian my understanding of sinning and plus forgiveness and repenting has grown and now becomes a thing that I recognise every day. The majority of the time when I sin, I ask for forgiveness and repent straight away. There are times when I forget and ask for forgiveness and repent when saying my daily prayers. Some of the sins I commit I may not recognise, especially if I am busy, and the sin is harder to notice. If I can explain to people what sinning is and encourage them to ask for forgiveness and repent from them, I will. The closer I am to God and the more his Holy Spirit is working in me the less likely I am to sin. God's Grace will also be trying to prevent me from sinning as well. There maybe occasions where I think I have sinned and I haven't. That can sometimes happen and as I am a Born Again Christian it is easier for me to think of small sins and be too critical about myself. Although Satan (i.e. The Devil) wants me to sin as much as I can, I know that having God's Grace with me throughout my life will prevent me sinning too often. God's doesn't want me to sin at all and nor do I. Knowing that I do sin and how to ask for forgiveness and knowing how to repent from these sins helps me so much. Being able to ask for forgiveness and truly repent from sins is a massive advantage in life. God will know at all times when I have sinned, when I have asked for forgiveness and when I have truly repented from the sins I have committed. When I do that as a Born Again Christian he will forgive me.

CHAPTER 25

Prayer

Another part of the gift of God's Grace is for us to be able to pray. Prayer is important in our lives and as long as it is genuine and we mean all we say then God will be listening to us. There are many things in our lives we can pray for. Prayer can be for things in our own lives and other people's lives that are difficult and when we and others are going through hard times. Prayer can be for things in our lives and other people's lives that are good and when we and others are going through good times, including exciting things in our lives. We can even pray to God when we are genuinely celebrating something. All prayer/praying needs to come from our heart and soul (the love and feelings we possess and God gives us), and we genuinely mean it. Knowledge of scripture/ the bible won't help when it comes to prayer/praying. Born Again Christians are used to praying most days and although they have many things to pray for the subjects do vary from one extreme to another. People pray for people who are ill, people in serious financial difficulty, people who are unemployed, people having personal problems and many other things. People can also pray for themselves. People also pray for exciting and good times including celebrating and winning. When we are praying we are always praying through Jesus Christ because he is the only one who died for our sins on the cross and he is our Saviour and Redeemer. The feelings and love that is in our heart and souls, and God provides us with, shows when we are praying whatever that prayer is about. Some people say different prayers at all different times during their daily lives, others have routine times and stick to similar prayers all the time. As long as the prayers Born Again Christians are all saying are genuine then God will be listening to all of them.

People who are not Born Again Christians and with no intentions of being so will find it hard to pray and will have no idea of what prayer means, and what it feels like to be listened to by God. When people are of another religion or no religion at all they are going to be praying to another so called god or idle, or not do any praying at all. The reason people are in this kind of situation is because they are being controlled by Satan (i.e. The Devil) and unfortunately they don't realise it. Satan (i.e. The Devil) is also preventing people from saying prayers and being listened to by the one and only true God. People who don't pray to the one and only true God have no heart and soul and don't realise what he has done and is doing for us. The amount of good in our lives that is provided by God is always going to win against the amount of bad in our lives provided by Satan (i.e. The Devil) if we are Born Again Christians. People who don't want to pray or pray to a fake god or idle and are part of another religion will need to be helped by Born Again Christians and explained to what praying to the one and only true God means. People who are praying to a fake god or idle and are of another religion won't be listened to by the one and only true God because they are not praying to him, so their prayers will count for nothing at the end of the day. Unfortunately all their prayers will be ignored and when Jesus Christ returns those prayers will only see them go with Satan (i.e. The Devil) to Hell. Only praying to the one and only true God will get them to Heaven.

Ever since I first started going to church and attending house group meetings/bible studies I have been praying. Regular prayers have been said at both services and house group meetings/bible studies. There is no exception of where and when prayers can be said and although I mainly say more prayers last thing at night when I am just getting into to bed I do say them at other times and places, especially when I am out and on my bicycle. I have prayed for many different things in the past and will keep on doing so in the future. During the hard times I have been through I have said prayers and some have been answered and some haven't as yet. Some of the prayers I said in the past took quite a long time to be answered but they were, including when I survived bowel cancer and am now pain free plus all the years I had epilepsy and after forty years I grew out of it. I have said prayers in the past so that I can obtain employment and although I have had jobs for short periods of time I am still looking for work and still have to attend jobcentre appointments, I still carry on praying because when a prayer hasn't been answered, as a Born Again Christian I know that God answers all prayers eventually, however long it takes. I have said prayers for good and exciting things that have happened in my life. When I was diagnosed with bowel cancer in 2000 and I had been sedated when I was operated on, I woke up and was told that I had my life saved. Through the prayers I said before I had the operation and God's

Grace being with me those prayers were answered. I have said prayers for many things including just before a job interview, just before and during a bowls match, just before and during a sponsored bike ride etc. It is not only prayers for myself I have said, I have said many prayers for other people as well and will carry on doing so. God's Grace helps me when I am praying.

CHAPTER 26

Peace

Through the gift of God's Grace, we also receive peace from our Lord because he wants us all to be living in peace. Born Again Christians all want our lives to be filled with peace. If we had peace all through our lives there would be no sin in the world. When going about their daily lives Born Again Christians have no intentions of disrupting, harming or sinning against others' lives and go about their daily lives in peace. Through living in peace many of the other gifts we receive such as love, kindness, joy etc. show in our lives. Peace is not only a wonderful part of God's Grace which Born Again Christians receive but it also gives us the feeling of freedom and shows in how Born Again Christians talk, behave, communicate and conduct themselves during and throughout their daily lives. Although Born Again Christians still sin during their lives most have the intention of keeping the peace and preventing domestics and arguments. Having the intention of keeping the peace during your life really does help and our Lord really does help us. Born Again Christians (also Jesus's Disciples) can also be used to help others to keep the peace during their daily lives plus also prevent problems even occurring on some occasions. Sometimes it will work and sometimes won't. One thing Born Again Christians pray for is peace and that applies to everyone with no exceptions made. The more peaceful the universe that

God created is the better. Born Again Christians will receive peace from God forever as long as they are true to their faith and maintain it forever. God's Holy Spirit will guide us as well. The strength that God provides us with throughout our lives will also help us to live a peaceful life and keep the peace. For most Born Again Christians living in peace and keeping the peace will mean a lot to them and to be able to make life easier for themselves and everyone else is just wonderful. It will also mean God is working in them.

For people who are not Born Again Christians and have no intentions of being so they will find it much harder to understand peace. Because of the presence of Satan (i.e. The Devil) people who don't believe in peace and keeping the peace will have no thought of it during their daily lives. How they talk, behave, communicate and conduct themselves during their daily lives won't matter to them even if they disrupt people's lives and cause domestics and arguments. Things such as hurting people, riots, protests, murders and other sins will take place as well. Satan (i.e. The Devil) will be trying his hardest to prevent people from believing in and keeping the peace. If people let Satan (i.e. The Devil) invade their lives and take control, the more likely they are to be disruptive and harmful to other people and the less likely they are to believe in the peace or keep the peace. People that do not believe in peace and want to carry on in that way will unfortunately end up with Satan (i.e. The Devil) in Hell. If people are hoping to change for the better then they need help from someone, preferably a Born Again Christian, and be explained about keeping the peace and what it means. For people who seriously want to change and believe in the peace and keep the peace it will take a fair bit of doing and the sooner it is put in to action the better. People who think they are believing in and keeping the peace and then find themselves not believing in or keeping the peace are not Born Again Christians. When people want to keep the peace during their lives it has to be a definite yes or no. There will be people who for them believing in peace and keeping the peace are just not in their nature and for them it is something they cannot adapt to. For people not wanting peace or to keep the peace, life will not only be a struggle for them but it will also make their own life harder and it will also make other people's lives harder as well. That also means they have no understanding of God's Grace and no intention of doing so either.

Before I became a Born Again Christian I was always one for keeping the peace. Since I have been attending church services and house groups I have learnt more and more about the peace. As a Born Again Christian my aim in my daily life is believing in peace and keeping the peace throughout the whole of my life. Whatever I may be doing and in whatever situation I am in keeping the peace and living a peaceful life is one of my priorities. It doesn't matter who I come in contact with and whatever is said or happens during my life I will still aim to keep the peace. If I have to at any time I will also help others to live a peaceful life and keep the peace. Offering other people peace when attending church services or at any other time is also a wonderful thing as long as it comes from the soul and is truly meant. I intend to keep the peace and live a peaceful life because God wants me to and with his Grace I will put that in to action and work on it every day. Although I have been through tough times in the past and some days have not been easy, depending on what is happening in my life, I always manage to keep the peace at home and wherever else I am. Feeling God's presence can also help me keep the peace and when I am near other people God's Holy Spirit is guiding me how I talk, behave, communicate and conduct myself during my daily life. It makes my life so much easier knowing that I intend to live a peaceful life and keep the peace with everyone. Even if meet people who are somewhat disruptive in how they behave and conduct themselves I either ignore them or try and calm them down and try and find a positive and peaceful outcome.

CHAPTER 27

Health

From birth until the day our bodies stop functioning on earth God wants our health to be as good as it can be. With God's Grace plus us understanding and accepting God's Grace our health will be as God wants our health to be. Our Lord actually wants our bodies to be perfect without a single health problem in our lives. Born Again Christians understand that keeping themselves healthy is not only important but something that God wants us to do because his Grace means wanting the very best for us. Throughout our daily lives we all suffer various things and our health is not as it should be because we don't have perfect bodies. The reason our health is not what it should be is nothing to do with God. Unfortunately, many people blame God for the problems with their bad health and forget that it is someone else that is causing the problems with their health. God is actually blameless. We also have a part to play in looking after ourselves and use our common sense in being healthy and staying healthy. What we eat and drink and the quantity of what we eat and drink can make a big difference in how healthy we are. The quality of both the food and drink can also make a difference. Another thing that could be a big factor in how healthy we are is making sure we keep as active as we can. This includes doing some form of exercise, whether it is walking, cycling, jogging or even some form of sport or activity. If we also stay away from things such as smoking, drugs, alcohol etc. and things that are likely to damage our health that will be a good thing.

For people who are not Born Again Christians and have no intentions of being so, understanding about God wanting us to be healthy and have a perfect body will be much harder for them to understand or accept because they do not believe in our Lord or accept or understand God's Grace either. Satan (i.e. The Devil) will be trying his hardest to make people who are not Born Again Christians think that whatever they eat and drink and whatever the quantity or quality it doesn't matter. He also wants them to consume whatever they want, however much it is and whatever causes those illnesses doesn't matter. Some people also disregard their lack of exercise and even disregard trying to keep themselves healthy in general as well. Satan (i.e. The Devil) is the one who people need to blame when it comes to suffering and having bad health at any time during their lives. People who don't know who his making them suffer and also causes the rest of their illnesses throughout their lives are unfortunately being caught out by Satan (i.e. The Devil) and will carry on doing so because of no faith or belief in the one and only true God. Whatever illnesses and bad health problems people are suffering from they have no chance of being saved by God unless they become Born Again Christians. The difference between people that understand God wants us to have a perfect body throughout our lives and those that blame him for all their illnesses and bad health is massive. That could be the difference between being in Heaven with God and being in Hell with Satan (i.e. The Devil).

Being a Born Again Christian myself and being through what I have been through has made me understand that God wants me to have a perfect body even though during my life on earth that won't be possible due to the presence of Satan (i.e. The Devil). Although I have been through epilepsy and bowel cancer for long periods of time I knew that all the time I was experiencing both of these illnesses/conditions that my Lord was with me all the time and that he would be using his power to prevent Satan (i.e. The Devil) getting to me more than he was able to. God knew that by me accepting the gift of his Grace that I would be accepting his help to overcome these illnesses/conditions. This also applies to all the other aches, pains and suffering I had, still have and have in the future. One thing I have had since 2015 has been sinus problems and how long I will have to endure that is unknown. I have also been careful throughout my life in what food and drinks I have consumed especially since the year 2001 when I was restricted to not eating certain things due to the bowel cancer I had. Part of God's Grace, which I receive every day of my daily life, includes knowing that I am going to be guided throughout my life, to look after myself, make sure that I stay healthy and that God will be with me all the time. I know that as part of staying healthy throughout my life I do things such as staying as mobile and active as possible. This includes things such as walking, cycling and playing bowls (both indoor and outdoor). I did this as part of my recovery from the after effects of bowel cancer. Having the feeling of my Lord being with me all the time and knowing that he has my best interests at heart, including my health, is an absolutely wonderful feeling. It means that God is close to me all the time as he is with other Born Again Christians and the amount of love he has for us is just unbelievably endless. There is nobody else in the world that can give us as much love and look after us more than God does. He wants the best including our health.

CHAPTER 28

Healing

Healing is a huge part of our lives and of God's Grace. For Born Again Christians and God being with them throughout their lives they have a huge advantage because of their faith, belief and trust in him. Because Born Again Christians are so close to God and want him with them all time they know that when they are ill, in pain and suffering God will be healing them. They could be healed instantly, within a few days, it maybe months, years or several decades. It could even be forever depending on what God is healing us from. Praying for God's healing of us is very important and he will be listening to us very carefully. The strength God has enables him to heal us. When it comes to how much God can do for us, including healing, there are no limitations. He can do anything to help us. It is his decision though and when we are healed it is up to God. As well as praying to God to be healed Born Again Christians also know that they need to be patient because being healed can take a long time in some cases. Because of what we go through during our lives being healed is so important and is also rewarding to us as well. The relief of being healed to some people is a massive thing and can make a huge difference to their lives. Sometimes Born Again Christians can feel on top of the world once they have been healed. Most people need to be healed from several things and find that they have only been healed from one. Being healed from one thing and not another is part of God's plan and most Born Again Christians find that they are healed from different things at different stages of their lives. Because Born Again Christians know that God is with them all the time the feeling of being healed is in them because they know at some time they will be healed. The day Jesus Christ returns and Born Again Christians go with him to Heaven they will be completely healed and will eventually have perfect bodies.

For people who are not Born Again Christians and have no intentions of being so the true meaning of being healed will be hard to understand. With very little or no understanding of or accepting God's Grace, being healed by God will not be something people who are not Born Again Christians understand. Because people who are not Born Again Christians are not praying to the one and only true God their prayers will not be heard or answered, whether they are praying for healing or not. Some never say prayers and don't have any intentions of doing so. Unfortunately for people who are not Born Again Christians God won't be healing them when they are ill, in pain and suffering. As a matter of fact, Satan (i.e. The Devil) will be trying his hardest to make their illnesses, pains and suffering even worse than it is. Some people who are not Born Again Christians have the idea that because they are unwell or suffering it will go away at some time and all will be okay. It may go away or temporarily go away but that isn't being healed by God. The day Jesus Christ returns, people who are not Born Again Christians will be left behind and will eventually be going with Satan (i.e. The Devil) to Hell and their idea of being healed will all be over. If people seriously and truly want to be healed they need to start having faith, trust and belief in the one and only true God and our saviour Jesus Christ.

As a Born Again Christian my understanding of God's healing through the gift of his Grace has been getting stronger and stronger as time has progressed. He has been with me all the way and has healed me from many things including epilepsy and bowel cancer. It took me forty years to be healed from the epilepsy I had and fifteen years to be healed from the bowel cancer. As well as saying prayers every day throughout these experiences I had to be patient and realise that God was with me all the time. Because of God's strength and power, he was able to heal me from any illnesses, pain and suffering in the past and will do so in the future. I am exceptionally grateful to God for all the healing he has given to me and because the strength and power he has is beyond what I or anyone else can imagine. God has also filled me with various things including mental and physical strength to endure and overcome the experiences I have been through. God knows that the strength he has filled me with is enough to overcome the bad experiences I have been through which have been caused by Satan (i.e. The Devil) and he knows that I have the faith, trust and belief in him to heal me and the day Jesus Christ returns I will be with him in Heaven and be completely healed. Whenever I need healing and I am saying prayers for that healing I very often feel the presence of God and know that he is working on me to be healed, whether it takes a short period of time or for a long time. God is even telling me to be strong, hang in there, be determined and not to worry whenever I am experiencing illnesses, pain and suffering in any way. For me, being healed by God is a wonderful thing and when it happened to me on various occasions in the past it gave me a great feeling that God is not only working on me but with his strength and power he is also trying to prevent Satan (i.e. The Devil) causing me any more bad experiences in the future.

CHAPTER 29

Glory

God himself is glory and everything he created and is still creating. Creating the heavens and the earth is part of God's glory as is creating mankind, all the animals and creatures in this world plus the whole of nature and wildlife. All the good in this world and all what God wanted and wants to create is all part of his glory. Having the unfortunate presence of Satan (i.e. The Devil) in this world meant another part of God's glory was deciding to have Jesus Christ (our Saviour) sacrifice his life on the cross (the resurrection) for the benefit of Born Again Christians to be given a second chance to live eternal life in a perfect world (Heaven) and living the kind of life we should have been living now. God wants us to live a perfect life and have perfect bodies but due to the presence of Satan (i.e. The Devil) we can't. Through the gift of God's Grace his glory shines through all Born Again Christians and will continue to do so. Born Again Christians are not only grateful for God's Grace but also his glory because it means so much and because of where they will be when we have the return of Jesus Christ. God's glory is also what he has planned for Born Again Christians when they arrive in Heaven. Because of his glory God knows who will be a Born Again Christian and who won't. God's glory is given to us by our Lord and he wants us to accept it and feel part of him, and that we are being looked after by him all the time. For people who are not yet Born Again Christians there is still time to convert to or become Born Again Christians and know what God's glory means. It may take some doing but it will be worth it. If people do want to become Born Again Christians, they don't want to take too long to make up their minds because it could be too late. Jesus Christ could return at any time and there is no way of telling when. It could be seconds away, months away, years away, decades and even centuries away. God's glory actually shines through this universe all the time.

People who are not Born Again Christians and have no intensions of being so will struggle to understand what God's glory is and will very often not want to know. Because of the presence of Satan (i.e. The Devil) it will make it harder still for people who are not Born Again Christians to realise that having God's glory in their lives would make a massive difference. Due to the attitudes, feelings and behaviour of people who are not Born Again Christians, Satan (i.e. The Devil) is going to make it extremely hard for them to accept and understand God's glory and what it means. People involved in other religions and even those of no religion at all are also going to find it hard to understand as well. Even people such as scientists will even come up with other ideas of how they were created and how the world first began without realising that it is all due to God's glory. For people who are not Born Again Christians their heart and souls are not with our Lord and their feelings for him and his glory just don't exist because they are letting the strength of Satan (i.e. The Devil) get to them. Not understanding and accepting the gift of God's Grace will also make it just as hard to understand and accept God's glory. Like Born Again Christians, people who are not Born Again Christians also have their lives created through God's glory and everything that is provided for them is what they require in God's eyes but understanding and accepting them is another matter. Receiving God's glory and knowing what it all means also includes knowing that God is blameless because he is perfect. Unfortunately, people who are not Born Again Christians, blame God on a regular basis, and for all different problems that occur in their lives. Without God's glory we wouldn't exist and couldn't live our lives as we do.

I, myself, am very grateful that through God's Grace I receive his glory and that I understand that he created me as he did this universe and all that live in this universe. I have been through hard times in my life but I know that through God's glory he wouldn't have wanted that for me or anyone else, and he knows that I know that through his glory I am going to cope with and overcome these hard times. He also knows that I know that what I have received in the past and receive in the future during my daily life is all through his glory. He is providing me with all the necessary things to live a normal life in his eyes and he knows that I know he is in control in my life and not Satan (i.e. The Devil). The strength, happiness, kindness, care, love etc. that I receive from God is all part of his glory which comes through me accepting and understanding the gift of his Grace. Knowing that I am part of God's glory is a wonderful feeling and that I am going to be able to live my daily life in his presence, and that he is with me all the time. It also means that when

Jesus Christ returns I will be with God in Heaven. For me, God's glory is a massive thing in anyone's life and knowing what it is, studying it, and finding out what the reward is from accepting and understanding it, is bigger than anything in this world.

CHAPTER 30

Light of the World

God's Grace also includes Jesus Christ being the light of the world and that means a lot to Born Again Christians because Jesus sacrificed his life on the cross (the resurrection) so that Born Again Christians have a second chance to live a perfect life in Heaven. Jesus Christ is also the light of world because if he hadn't sacrificed his life on the cross we would have had no chance to have eternal life in Heaven or live a perfect life. God the Father knew what was going to happen and that he would need to plan for Jesus Christ to sacrifice his life on the cross due to the presence of Satan (i.e. The Devil) before he rose again and joined him Heaven and his right hand side. The fact that Jesus Christ died for us on the cross was due to the sins which we commit it means he is our Saviour and hero, and we only commit these sins due to the presence of Satan (i.e. The Devil). Born Again Christians not only know that Jesus Christ is their Saviour and hero but they pray to him for this reason on a regular basis. It is not only important to them but it means so much. Jesus Christ also knows who is a Born Again Christian and who is trying to spread the word, and is one of his disciples. Believing in Jesus Christ and realising he is the light of the world is a massive thing but it is also one of the most important things for Born Again Christians. As well as Jesus Christ being our Saviour and hero Born Again

Christians know that in Heaven it will be complete light.

For people who are not Born Again Christians and have no intentions of being so, Jesus Christ (the light of the world) does not exist. Although the presence of Satan (i.e. The Devil) exists in all of us because we all sin, people who are not Born Again Christians will not realise this or recognise these sins, and will think they don't matter. Unfortunately for people who are not Born Again Christians and have no intentions of being so they will never get to see the light of the world and will be looking forward to utter darkness in Hell along with Satan (i.e. The Devil). With very little or no faith, trust and belief in Jesus Christ (the light of the world) their lives are going to be very bleak and when it comes to being in Hell along with Satan (i.e. The Devil) their lives are going to be the worst they can possibly be. Satan (i.e. The Devil) brings utter darkness to people's lives. The day Jesus Christ returns, for people who are not Born Again Christians, there will be no going back and it will be too late to change. The difference between the light of the world (Jesus Christ) in Heaven and utter darkness with Satan (i.e. The Devil) in Hell is massive. There are no other extremes in this universe bigger than these. For people who are not Born Again Christians, not wanting to believe in Jesus Christ (the light of the world), it will be a massive mistake because of where they are going to end up and what their lives are going to be like in utter darkness in Hell. The same applies to all the people who are not Born Again Christians who do not believe that Jesus Christ sacrificed his life on the cross (the resurrection) for all of us due to our sins.

Personally, Jesus Christ is the light of the world and for me I understand that without him sacrificing his life on the cross for me I wouldn't have the chance to be able to live a perfect life in Heaven when Jesus returns. It means so much to me to know that Jesus is the light of the world because it gives me hope, positivity, happiness and all the good things that are included in the gift of God's Grace, which I receive all the time. The fact that Jesus Christ is the light of the world makes me feel so positive during my daily life because of what I have to look forward to and that being in Heaven with him is going to be that good, there is nothing better in this world. It also makes life for me easier when I have been through or go through hard times and face problems at any time. God also knows that I know that Jesus Christ is the light of the world and means a lot to me. Being the light of the world means Jesus Christ is shining on me all the time as he is all other Born Again Christians. Because I am a Born Again Christian and with Jesus Christ (the light of the world) shining on me, it also makes it easier for me to explain and talk to other people about my faith and gives me more confidence as time goes by. The fact that Jesus Christ is the light of the world makes me feel more important as one of Jesus Christ's disciples and I am able to spread the word. The feeling of knowing that Jesus Christ (the light of the world) is going to return at some time is not only a wonderful and exciting feeling for me but what I have got to look forward to in Heaven is just unimaginable at the present time. Having that kind of feeling in me and thinking of having a perfect life sometimes makes me feel on top of the world.

CHAPTER 31

Holy Communion

For Born Again Christians receiving Holy Communion means a lot and is very important to them. Receiving the bread and wine is receiving it in remembrance of Jesus Christ our Saviour. Through the gift of God's Grace, we are able to receive the bread and wine and put our heart and soul in to knowing that Jesus Christ sacrificed his life for us. The bread is representing Jesus Christ's body and the wine is representing his blood. Sacrificing his life on the cross (the resurrection) not only means a lot but it is the biggest sacrifice in this universe ever made, and it was all done because of the sins of this world, caused by Satan (the Devil), and to give Born Again Christians a chance to live a perfect life in Heaven. Born Again Christians take Holy Communion mainly on a regular basis and seriously, and it is close to their heart and soul because of what Jesus Christ did for them. Through sacrificing his life on the cross, Jesus Christ is showing complete and perfect love towards us all but only Born Again Christians recognise this. Jesus Christ's body was broken for us so that our broken bodies can be fixed by him. Born Again Christians bodies will be fixed because of their faith, belief and trust in him. Jesus Christ sacrificing his life on the cross was all part of God's plan to give Born Again Christians the chance of living a perfect life in Heaven, this was part of God's plan because of the existence of Satan (i.e. The Devil). Each time Born Again Christians receive Holy Communion God realises this and knows how close they are to Jesus Christ because of his sacrifice on the cross and knows in their heart and soul how much it means. Receiving Holy Communion is very important because receiving the bread and wine is not only representing Jesus body and blood but is also representing the biggest event that ever happened in this universe.

For people who are not Born Again Christians and have no intentions of being so, not understanding or accepting God's Grace will make it very hard for them to know what Holy Communion is and what it means as well. Due to the presence of Satan (i.e. The Devil) people who are not Born Again Christians will not want to know our saviour Jesus Christ and will have no understanding of what he did on the cross (the resurrection). Unfortunately, people who are not Born Again Christians will not realise that what Jesus Christ did on the cross was for everyone including themselves but with no faith, belief or trust in him they have no chance of being with him in Heaven. For people not receiving Holy Communion and not understanding the meaning of it or ever wanting to, life is going to be much worse for them when they are in the hands of Satan (i.e. The Devil) in Hell. People who are not Born Again Christians don't even realise or believe that Jesus Christ sacrificing his life on the cross (the resurrection) was the biggest event to happen in this universe. Not receiving Holy Communion is going to be a massive loss to people who are not Born Again Christians. For people who are not Born Again Christians the presence of our Lord will not be with them and not receiving Holy Communion either will see the presence of our Lord not being with them. Because they are letting the presence of Satan (i.e. The Devil) get to them big time, the presence of God is very unlikely going to be with them.

Personally, I have received Holy Communion at various church services since the early 1980's. Each time I have received it I have got the feeling of my Lord's presence in me and understand that I am receiving it because of what it means and that Jesus Christ sacrificed his life for me. I understand and know that each time I consume the bread and wine it is representing Jesus Christ's body and blood. For Jesus Christ to die on the cross (the resurrection) for me and because of the sins I have committed during my life is something really important to me because it gives me a chance as a Born Again Christian to live my life in Heaven when Jesus Christ returns. I am so fortunate to be a Born Again Christian and have eternal life even though it is part of God's plan and was well before I was born. Although all church services are important Holy Communion services are the more important. One quote from the bible and from the chapter of Luke 22, verses 19 and 20 is; And he took bread, gave thanks and broke it, and gave it to them, saying, "This is my body given for you, do this in remembrance of me." In the same way, after the supper he took the cup, saying, "This cup is the new covenant in my blood, which is poured out for you." Just like us, Jesus Christ's body, as a human being, consists of flesh and bones, and blood. The sacrifice that Jesus Christ made for me on the cross (the resurrection) is the biggest thing in the universe that could ever happen in my life because it means that although Satan (i.e. The

Devil) wants me to continually sin I am receiving God's Grace and that is helping me to realise that what Jesus Christ did for me is more important than anything, and is giving me the chance of life in Heaven and a perfect life. It is also the love that Jesus Christ is showing me because of him sacrificing his life. It means so much to me and nobody else in this universe can do anything like Jesus Christ did. It's just impossible.

CHAPTER 32

Devotion

God's devotion in us is 100% perfect, continuous, and has no ending. It is another important part of his Grace as well. He is devoted to Born Again Christians all the time. From well before we were born, throughout our earthly lives and for Born Again Christians throughout our heavenly lives. It doesn't matter what is happening in our lives and whatever situation we are in God is there for us all. He knows when we are going through good times and hard times. His devotion to us is to provide us with his complete love for us and as much good as possible. He wants our lives to be perfect but there is one thing in our lives that prevents that. Born Again Christians understand that God is devoted to them throughout their lives and most of them can feel his presence in them while they go about their daily lives. The devotion that God gives us is so important and such a big thing only Born Again Christians will understand. The strength and power of God's devotion to us is so big because he not only wants the best for us but he also wants to prevent bad things happening to us, which includes preventing us making wrong decisions. He is also devoted to helping us when we are going through hard times and trying to make a recovery or making some form of progress in life. Born Again Christians are more likely to make a recovery or some form of progress in life because they know that God is devoted to them and with them all the time. It means while they are saying prayers they will be answered at some time and things will gradually improve through their own faith and God's devotion to them. God's devotion to us includes answering our prayers even if they are not instantly.

For people who are not Born Again Christians, due to lack of or no faith, belief and trust in him, God is not devoted to them and will be very hard for them to understand. Unfortunately, due to the presence of Satan (i.e. The Devil), people who are not Born Again Christians will not realise or feel God's devotion to them during their daily lives. God is actually devoting his life to making people's lives the best ever but due to the presence of Satan (i.e. The Devil) people who are not Born Again Christians are ignoring him and making a huge mistake. As a matter of fact, they are letting Satan (i.e. The Devil) devote himself to them and letting him provide as much bad or wickedness in them as he can. Because they have no faith, trust and belief in God they are letting Satan (i.e. The Devil) take full control and his devotion to them is working all the more and will be much worse for them. Accepting Satan's (i.e. The Devil's) devotion to them will be like accepting a journey in to Hell. Refusing the best in life you can be given is something nobody should be doing, especially when it comes to God's devotion to us via his Grace, and is a big mistake. It is a massive thing when it comes to ignoring God, having no faith, belief and trust in him and having no feelings for him. It sounds and is evil because Satan (i.e. The Devil) is causing this to happen to all people who are not Born Again Christians and they are not realising what good God would have been doing for them through his devotion.

For myself, I know that God's devotion to me is there all the time and will be forever. He has shown his devotion to me through good times and hard times, whatever my situation has been and still is. The feeling I get during my daily life is that God's devotion to me is travelling with me, everywhere I go and in whatever I am involved in. His devotion is guiding me in the right direction and is telling me that whenever I sin I will recognise it and I will either ask for forgiveness and repent immediately or not long after when I am saying my prayers. Because God's devotion to me is part of his Grace his devotion is a free gift and is part of him showing his love and looking after me throughout my life. Because God is showing his devotion to me I am feeling his presence plus he is keeping hold of me all the time. I get the feeling of his arms round me and hugging me because his devotion to me is exceptionally good. God's devotion to me also means he knows that my faith, belief and trust in him is exceptionally strong and I am with him all the time. God's devotion to me included being with me through some hard times such as when I had forty years of epilepsy and nearly fifteen years of bowel cancer and the after effects. God followed me throughout those years and knew well before I was born that I was going to eventually recover and through his devotion to me that I would have the strength via his Grace to make progress, cope and completely overcome them. This has also applied to other situations including all the years I have found it hard to find employment plus times when I have been unwell with other health problems. God's devotion to me is not only exceptionally special but I know it will be with me all the time and forever. I have eternal life as a Born Again Christian and God's devotion to me is eternal as well. God's promises to me, like his devotion, as to other Born Again Christians, will always be kept and never broken. That is special.

CHAPTER 33

Blessed

For Born Again Christians being blessed means so much to them because it is God showing his love towards them, guiding them, protecting them and many other things to see they live as good a life as they can. For Born Again Christians it is a wonderful thing because they can go about their daily lives knowing they are blessed as part of God's Grace and that wonderful feeling helps them because it makes life easier. The thought and feeling of being blessed is so good it makes Born Again Christians so grateful to God for what he has done and is doing for them. The understanding of being blessed is just as important as the other things included in God's Grace. As Born Again Christians go about their daily lives God is not only with them all the time but he is blessing them all the time. With God's blessing there is no limit to the good he wants for them and that includes whenever they are going through hard times and things are tough. Part of being blessed is giving them strength and faith to keep going, however hard things maybe. When Born Again Christians know they are blessed they are not only praying for that but putting it in action when they go about their daily lives. God is also blessing Born Again Christians so they can show their love towards others including people who they have forgiven because of their sinning against them. God blesses Born Again Christians in so many ways it would be hard to name everything plus it endless. Whilst God is blessing all Born Again Christians he is also following them throughout their lives and making sure they receive the best they possibly can. He wants nothing less than perfection for them all and that is part of him blessing them. Being blessed means that when Born Again Christians go about their daily lives and they know they are not sinning they have nothing to worry about or fear. They just need to keep calm and relax as much as possible. Born Again Christians can live a blessed life through God's blessing.

God is not blessing people who are not Born Again Christians because of their lack of or no faith, trust or belief in him, plus they will have no understanding or idea that they are not being blessed. Because Satan (i.e. The Devil) is taking control of the lives of people who are not Born Again Christians they will find it exceptionally hard or virtually impossible to know or feel God's blessings. This will not only make life harder, with no understanding of God's blessings, but it also means that Satan (i.e. The Devil) will also being taking control of people's feelings, thoughts, words and general behaviour during their daily lives. People who are not Born Again Christians are also going to be rejecting God's blessings for them as well as other parts of God's Grace and that will make life for them much worse. People who are not Born Again Christians are not understanding that in rejecting God, including his blessing, and being controlled by Satan (i.e. The Devil) they are rejecting the best they can receive and accepting the worst. That means accepting the worst kind of life that is being offered and that will be a life with Satan (i.e. The Devil) in Hell. Because

God is not blessing people who are not Born Again Christians, that could go on forever and is endless, and unfortunately for them they are ignoring him and are doing themselves no good at all. Because they have no understanding of his blessing and don't want to, the love, guidance, protection and many other things from God's blessing will be rejected and will find the opposite happening to them because of Satan (i.e. The Devil) being in control.

For me, personally, being blessed by God means so much and is a big part of my life, and I am glad it is. Not only is God blessing me but it is in me throughout the whole of my daily life, and it doesn't matter wherever I may have been or will be in the future, or whatever I have been involved in the past or will be involved in in the future. God's blessing me throughout my life has made a real difference to me because he keeps me calm and relaxed whatever my situation is. His blessing also makes me very positive and makes my faith, belief and trust in him exceptionally strong. His blessing also guides and protects me all the time and throughout my eternal life. It makes life for me so much easier knowing that God is blessing me all the time. I know that God wants the best for me and wants perfection for me as well. He knows that until Jesus Christ returns my life won't be perfect due the presence of Satan (i.e. The Devil). God's blessing me also prevents me looking at things negatively or worrying about things, this included all the years I was affected by epilepsy, bowel cancer and long term unemployment. Even in the worst situations I have been in, having God's blessing has been an enormous help to prevent me worrying or being nervous. It makes me so thankful and grateful for God's blessing to me because it is a huge part of his Grace and is a free gift from him as well. Having that feeling of God being with me all the time and blessing me is not only so wonderful but also in my mind it is like safety and security with me all the time. God has also blessed me with the biggest blessing of all times and that is that Jesus Christ, who is my Saviour, died on the cross and sacrificed his life for me because of all the sins I have committed during my life and he will return again and take me up to Heaven due to the fact I am a Born Again Christian.

CHAPTER 34

Harmony

For Born Again Christians harmony is one thing that is experienced during their daily lives on a regular basis because as well as having faith, belief and trust in God they know he is with them all the time and they can feel him in them, around them and wherever they maybe. It is a wonderful thing to know that God is following all those that truly have faith, belief and trust in him and that he is living with them all the time. The harmony with God in a Born Again Christian's life is like a bond and continues forever, whatever is happening in their lives. A Born Again Christian knows that because they are receiving God's Grace the harmony with God is not only going to be with them all the time but it is like having complete love and safety with our Lord. Born Again Christians are grateful and thankful for receiving God's Grace and that includes the harmony with him. Being in harmony with God means he is also guiding us wherever we go and whatever we do. Born Again Christians are with God and being in harmony with him means although they sin they know when they have sinned and have to ask for forgiveness and repent from those sins. Being in harmony with God all the time is essential but only Born Again Christians are able to do this. Another reason Born Again Christians are in harmony with God is because he is providing them with the very best they can possibly receive. With their love and faith in Jesus

Christ their Saviour they will also be in harmony with God. Being in harmony with God, means Born Again Christians have little or nothing to worry about during their daily lives.

For people who are not Born Again Christians being in harmony with God is not possible. Having very little or no faith, belief and trust in God means not being in harmony with him and is the same as deserting him. It means people who are not Born Again Christians are in harmony with Satan (i.e. The Devil) and the majority of them don't even realise it. God is providing them with the best they can ever receive in their lives but unfortunately for them they are not in harmony with him and are ignoring him plus letting Satan (i.e. The Devil) take control of their lives. It means that during their daily lives communicating, behaving and being in control of themselves is going to be a lot harder because of not being in harmony with God. Satan (i.e. The Devil) will be preventing people who are not Born Again Christians being in harmony with God for as long as he possibly can, most of them forever. Because he is that evil Satan (i.e. The Devil) is in harmony with so many people who are not Born Again Christians and they don't realise or know it. Because people are in harmony with Satan (i.e. The Devil) they are being lead in the wrong direction all the time and have no idea of their sins they are committing throughout their lives. When people are in harmony with Satan (i.e. The Devil) all kinds of evil and wicked words, thoughts and ideas will be going through their minds and they end up getting acted upon and all kinds of things are thought, said and done that shouldn't be and God will know this. If harmony with Satan (i.e.

The Devil) can be avoided and prevented it will be the best thing ever in an individual's life. A person who is not a Born Again Christian and who is in harmony with the evil one is going to end up living eternal life with Satan (i.e. The Devil) in Hell. Nobody wants that.

For myself, I am in harmony in God all the time and will carry on being so. It means so much to me to be in harmony with God because he is looking after me and making my life so much easier. It doesn't mean life for me is completely easy because I have been through many hard times and suffered in the past plus I have sinned many times as well. Because of God's harmony in me it makes it easier as a Born Again Christian to know when I have sinned and how to put up with and cope with pain and suffering of different kinds. What I have been through in the past has given me a slight advantage and having had experience of hard times and suffering which included forty years of epilepsy, fifteen years of bowel cancer and after effects plus long periods of unemployment as well. Because of being in harmony with God he has been with me and guided me throughout many situations during my daily life and will continue to be so. The feeling of being in harmony with God is like him having his arms round me all the time, carrying me wherever I go and being my safety and security throughout my life. Being in harmony with God means I have no need to worry, be scared or panic about anything and to stay calm and relaxed in all situations. It also means that I am in harmony with God because my faith, belief and trust in him is not only strong but it can also be felt. It is the same with being in Harmony with Jesus Christ and the Holy Spirit as well. All are God and all are as important to me as each other. The harmony I have with God means I will be able to live through good times and not so good times, and be able to cope with anything. God knows that I am in harmony with him and that it will also prevent Satan (i.e. The Devil) taking control of my life.

CHAPTER 35
Discipleship

When Born Again Christians receive God's Grace they will also be delivering discipleship to others. People who are Born Again Christians are also disciples and spread the word of God (the bible) as much as they possibly can, so that people who have yet to become Christians can find out about the word of God (the bible) and learn about it for their own benefit. One disciple of God can make a huge difference to another person's life by telling them about scripture (the bible) and what the importance of what Jesus Christ did for us all and why. When a person converts to being a Born Again Christian through another Born Again Christian speaking to them about scripture (the bible) and what the importance of what Jesus Christ did for us all and why, then the disciple has done his or her job, and God will be very pleased with them. For people who are Born Again Christians and disciples of God it is a wonderful feeling to know that being a disciple is not only an important job but it can make the difference between someone living in Heaven and someone living in Hell. Because disciples cannot force someone to believe in God and in Christianity nobody is forced to believe but disciples are spreading God's word to non-believers for their own good and because it is the difference between living in Heaven and living in Hell. Born Again Christians are not only keen to spread God's word (scripture) but they know it is a massive thing if someone converts to being a Born Again Christian. Disciples are doing their jobs and spreading God's word because their hearts and souls are telling them that what God through Jesus Christ the Saviour has done and is doing for them needs to be passed on to others who are not yet accepting it. Some people do listen and eventually convert to being a Born Again Christian but there a lot of people who don't listen and never will. That is unfortunate for the person/people that don't accept God's word but that doesn't mean the disciple hasn't done their job.

For people who are not Born Again Christians and have no intentions of being so, being a disciple of God is not possible. Satan (i.e. The Devil) is making them his disciples and that means creating more problems and spreading more bad and evil in this universe. Being a disciple of Satan (i.e. The Devil) will really make life hard for people who are not Born Again Christians, whether they are of another religion or of no religion at all, it certainly won't work. Because Satan (i.e. The Devil) is leading people who are not Born Again Christians in the wrong direction he is also encouraging them to be a disciple for him plus think, say and do as much bad or evil to others as possible. Most people who are not Born Again Christians and never will be, don't realise they are closer to being a disciple for Satan (i.e. The Devil) because they are not with God. In this universe every person that is created by God is either with him or against him, and nothing in between. As well as ignoring and rejecting what true disciples of God are telling them about scripture (the bible) people who are not Born Again Christians are getting closer to Satan (i.e. The Devil) as time goes by, and if they carry on in that way it will make it harder and harder for them. People who are not Born Again Christians are not accepting God and what Jesus Christ did for them by sacrificing his life on the cross for the sins of the world and are rejecting him. By rejecting him it means they don't have faith, belief and trust in him and are doing what Satan (i.e. The Devil) wants them to do.

As time has gone by my faith and discipleship for my Lord has got stronger and stronger and will carry on being so. Whether I have been through good times or hard times in my life, my discipleship for my Lord will always keep going. Because I am a Born Again Christian my love for everyone in this universe (love thy neighbour as thyself) means I am hoping that my discipleship will have some effect on people and converting them to being Born Again Christians. My love for everyone in this universe and hoping they become Born Again Christians is going to be a massive benefit to those people because they will not only receive God's love but they will be accepting his Grace and understanding what Jesus Christ did for them when he sacrificed his life on the cross all because of their sins. If my discipleship converts someone in to being a Born Again Christian it means God's love in me is helping another person to live their life in Heaven rather than Hell. If anyone converts to being a Born Again Christian through something I told them about scripture (the bible) then it gives me a wonderful feeling because I will have done a job that God is very pleased with. Helping someone convert to being a Born Again Christian is a massive thing for that person who converts. Because I am one of Jesus Christ's disciples there is no limit to whom in this universe I spread God's word (scripture/the bible) to if it converts them to becoming a Born Again Christian. Being one of Jesus Christ's disciples also gives me a lift during my daily life and it not only helps me in my life in general but it also helps me when I need to speak to people about God's word (scripture/the bible) and what it means and what a difference it would make to them if they were a Born Again Christian. Getting a person to convert to being a Born Again Christian may take a lot of doing but it is all down to the person who has been told about God's word whether or not they believe in it or not.

CHAPTER 36
Welcome

Welcoming us in to his world is also part of God's Grace and as a free gift (God's Grace) it means he wants us in his world all the time. Born Again Christians know that when they are eventually in Heaven (eternal life) with their Lord they will have already been welcomed in to his kingdom. Born Again Christians also know that during their earthly life (also eternal life) God is welcoming them all the time and through their faith, belief and trust in him they understand and accept his welcoming in to his kingdom. Welcoming people in to his kingdom is a continuous thing for God and it is a huge pleasure for our Lord to be welcoming people in to his kingdom. The more people our Lord can welcome in to his kingdom the better. Being welcomed in to God's kingdom is a massive thing. During a Born Again Christian's daily life God is welcoming them in to his kingdom all the time. It doesn't matter what situation they are in or whatever is happening to them he is always there to welcome them. To know that God is welcoming them in to their lives every day is a big advantage to Born Again Christians because it gives them a good feeling and makes them think of him being with them in any situation. Being welcomed by God is a great comfort and a great feeling to all Born Again Christians because they know he is in control of everything that is happening in the world. For Born Again Christians being welcomed by God in to his kingdom is the same as being welcomed in to the best place they will ever be and being welcomed in to the only place of perfection in the world and a place where they will eventually be living their lives in Heaven.

Whilst God welcomes everyone in to his kingdom continuously through his Grace, people who are not Born Again Christians don't understand or accept the fact that God wants to welcome them in to his kingdom but they are rejecting him and ignoring him because they have no faith, belief and trust in him. Satan (i.e. The Devil) will be doing his very best and trying to prevent people from being welcomed in to God's kingdom. He will be trying to welcome as many people as possible in to his kingdom. People who are not Born Again Christians will easily be welcomed in to the kingdom of Satan (i.e. The Devil) which will eventually lead them to living with him in Hell. More and more people, as time goes by, are being welcomed by Satan (i.e. The Devil) in to his kingdom and not realising it. The welcoming by Satan (i.e. The Devil) in to his kingdom is influencing people very easily because of having no faith, belief and trust in God plus how they behave, talk and their attitude throughout their lives. Being welcomed in to the kingdom of Satan (i.e. The Devil) is not only a massive mistake by anyone but not knowing where it will eventually lead them to is an even bigger mistake. Having a life in Hell is going to be having a life with someone who is pure evil. God knows well before people are born who is going to accept his welcoming in to his kingdom and who is going to reject him and be part of the kingdom of Satan (i.e. The Devil). By rejecting God's welcome in to his world people who are not Born Again Christians are also preventing themselves living a life of perfection in Heaven.

God welcomed me in to his world and as a Born Again Christian I understand and accept his welcome because I know that through God's son Jesus Christ (my Saviour and Redeemer) I am living eternal life on earth and in Heaven plus I will be living a life of perfection in Heaven when Jesus Christ returns. God is continuously welcoming me in to his world and I am accepting his welcome throughout my daily life. I am accepting God's welcome because it is so important to me and what it means to me. Knowing that God is welcoming me in to his kingdom gives me a different feeling each day during my life. It fills me with positivity, joy, discipleship, devotion, friendship, love and many other positive things that are part of God's Grace. Knowing that I am welcomed in to God's kingdom also makes me feel calm and relaxed, and it also makes me know that I have nothing to worry about or to be fearful of. Because God is welcoming me in to his kingdom he is giving me the chance to have eternal life in Heaven through his son Jesus Christ sacrificing his life for me because of the sins I have committed. God knows that I am sorry for them and have asked for forgiveness, and repented from them, and will do so in the future when necessary. Being welcomed in to God's kingdom is also the best thing in the world that will ever happen to anyone and I am glad I understand it and accept God's welcome. For me, to think and know that I am going to live a life in Heaven with a perfect body, to live a life in complete peace and love and all through the resurrection of Jesus Christ, it is something I am going accept immediately without any doubt, and this also comes from God welcoming me in to his kingdom. Being welcomed in to God's kingdom to me is much different to being welcomed in to anywhere else in the world. Entering the kingdom of Heaven is going to be a spectacular welcome because of what it is like and what it all means. I am certainly going to be looking forward to the welcome I get as will other Born Again Christians. The rest of my life will be in Heaven then.

CHAPTER 37

The Trinity

The Trinity is a massive part of God's Grace and for Born Again Christians it means so much to them. God the Father created the world including the heavens and the earth plus all of human mankind. God the Son (Jesus Christ) was resurrected and died on the cross, sacrificed his life for all our sins, rose again and is currently in Heaven, sitting at the right hand of God the Father. God the Holy Spirit is with us all the time and is guiding us throughout our earthly lives. Born Again Christians know that there is only one true God in this world and each part of God is just as important as the other. To be living our lives in this world God the Father (one part of the Trinity) would need to create where we are living but also create us as human beings as well. God's strength and power is enough to create the earth and human mankind, plus he is in control of the world as well. Unfortunately, we had Satan (The Devil), who was a fallen angel, in this world, and thought he was stronger and more powerful than God, and has tempted all humans and created sin and evil all over the world including today. None of us need sin and evil taking place in this world because when God the Father created the world he promised us peace and perfection. God the Son (Jesus Christ and second part of the Trinity) was not only born through Mary but also sacrificed his life on the cross. He did it because of the sins we commit and he did it for all Born Again Christians so that we have a chance of living the life that God the Father promised us plus when Born Again Christians enter Heaven. God the Holy Spirit (the third part of the Trinity) was sent by Jesus Christ to be a helper to all of us during our lives on earth. The Holy Spirit is with us all the time throughout the whole of our lives and Born Again Christians know that he is with them all the time.

People who are not Born Again Christians and have no intentions of being so, will not understand what the Trinity is and what it stands for or means. Satan (The Devil) will be part of most people's lives but for non-believers he will be part of their lives more of the time than with Born Again Christians. With no belief, trust and faith in our Lord they will struggle to realise that God the Father, God the Son and God the Holy Spirit are the Trinity and the one and only God in this world. Most will not realise that the world they are living in plus their own bodies were created by God the Father. Most will not realise that God the Son (Jesus Christ) died for their sins and sacrificed his life on the cross so that they have a chance to live a perfect life in Heaven and instead they will be heading for Hell with Satan (The Devil). Most will not realise that Jesus Christ sent a helper, known as the God the Holy Spirit, who exists in the world and is guiding those who are believers. Because non-believers have no faith, belief and trust in our Lord their understanding that God is three-in-one will not come to them and it will be hard for them to accept. They won't realise that each part is as important as each other. Non-believers' souls for God the Father, God the Son and God the Holy Spirit just don't exist because Satan (The Devil) has taken control of them and they have no idea.

Personally, the Trinity means so much to me because as a Born Again Christian I not only need the Trinity but each part of it is as important as each other. For me to be living my life and to be brought in to this world, God the Father had to create the world and create all mankind including myself. Because of this I am very grateful because I am living a life that God has provided me with. It means I am one of God's children, I am related to him and I am very close to him. Each day of my daily life I am thinking about how much it means because of being part of God's world and that he is my creator. God the Son (Jesus Christ) is just as important to me because he sacrificed his life on the cross because of all the sins I commit and he has given me a chance through me asking for forgiveness and repenting from my sins of living my life in Heaven plus living a perfect life. If Jesus Christ hadn't been born and never existed, I would have had no chance of living a life in Heaven and living a perfect life because of the presence of Satan (The Devil). Because I am a Born Again Christian I am one of Jesus Christ's disciples and I try my best to spread the word and let non-believers know about him, and why he is so important to me. God the Holy Spirit is also a big part of me because he is with me all the time during my earthly life, every day of my daily life. God the Father and God the Son (Jesus Christ) are at present in Heaven whilst God the Holy Spirit is everywhere including on earth. God the Holy Spirit is guiding me throughout my daily life and is pointing me in the right direction and looking after me no matter what happens in my life. God the Holy Spirit is as important as God the Father and God the Son (Jesus Christ) because his presence is there all the time and I can feel the support I am receiving throughout my life.

CHAPTER 38

Friendship

For Born Again Christians God's friendship to them is exceptionally important and is ongoing forever. The friendship between a Born Again Christian and God means so much to them because they know what he has done for them, what he is doing for them now and what he will be doing for them in the future. It is an ongoing closeness and is very personal because it makes their daily lives so much easier. As well feeling the closeness of God, Born Again Christians know that God himself wants the friendship between him and all his disciples/Born Again Christians to continue forever. The friendship Born Again Christians receive from God is through his Grace and he wants them to feel the friendship in the same way. It has to work both ways for it to be a complete success. Born Again Christians want their friendship with God to work and be a success and they are determined to make it work. Because of the presence of Satan (The Devil) the friendship between God and all the humans in this world isn't perfect. Born Again Christians are able to overcome that problem and make sure their friendship with God works because the free gift of his Grace to them helps to keep the friendship going whatever is happening in their lives. The friendship between Born Again Christians and God is also completely genuine and also the love between the two. The soul and spirit that Born Again Christians have works as part of their friendship towards God. Born Again Christians friendship towards God in most cases grows and grows plus gets stronger and stronger as times moves on. The friendship for God (including the Father, Son and Holy Spirit) not only means so much but it is for the most important person in creation and for the one who sacrificed their life for all of mankind. The friendship God has with all Born Again Christians also means so much to him as well.

People who are not Born Again Christians and have no intentions of being so will find it hard to have a friendship with God or not even want to have a friendship with God. Because of Satan (The Devil) being a big part of their lives and taking control of them he will be leading people who are not Born Again Christians further away from God and that will prevent people having a friendship with God. The feelings of friendship between a non-believer and God are non-existent. Non-believers' feelings, attitudes, behaviour and general reactions during their daily lives will play a big part in working out if they really have a friendship with God or not. Their friendship will unfortunately for them be with Satan (The Devil) and they don't even realise it. Some non-believers try and make out they have a friendship with God but unfortunately due their lack of or no faith, belief and trust in him it won't work. Not understanding and accepting God's Grace will make it harder because it means they are being offered his friendship and they are refusing it and it means they don't want to know him or believe in him. As time progresses non-believers are going to find it harder and harder to have a friendship with God because of having no faith, belief and trust in him and not wanting to. Their disbelief is going to get stronger as time goes by especially if they are of another religion. With all the things that are happening in the world and a lot of the unfortunate events taking place a lot of non-believers will be blaming God for them and not realising he has nothing to do with all the bad and evil things that are happening in this world. Satan (The Devil) is responsible for all the bad and evil things happening in this world and the idea of blaming God for them will also prevent a friendship with him.

My personal friendship with God has been going on for many years and as time has progressed it has been getting stronger and stronger. That means so much to me and it will mean a lot to God as well. During my daily life I am not only with him but I am also thinking of him, talking to him and praying to him. My close friendship and feelings for God have for many years made me feel I can feel God's arms round my shoulders and giving me a friendship hug on quite a few occasions. It is a wonderful feeling to have plus the closeness between us. I am determined as a Born Again Christian to keep this close friendship with God going. It also includes my close friendship with Jesus Christ because of what he did for me when he sacrificed his life for me because of my sins and because of giving me a second chance to live my life in Heaven and live a perfect life. To have a friendship with God is the best thing in the world and for me I couldn't ask for anything better. A friendship with anyone is important to me but to have one with God is not only the best but is absolutely wonderful as I am one of his children and he created me and the universe I am living in. The friendship I have with God will not only exist during my earthly life but it will continue in to when I am living with him in Heaven. The power and glory of God's Grace will not only be with me forever but it will also prevent Satan (The Devil) getting in the way of my friendship with God. He will be trying as hard as possible to end my friendship with God but I know and God knows that Satan (The Devil) will eventually fail at his attempt to end my friendship with God.

CHAPTER 39

Humbleness & Humility

In receiving God's Grace Born Again Christians understand that during their daily lives they need to show humbleness and humility and not go above and beyond what God wants them to or to try and be someone who they are not. They understand that humbleness and humility will help them and will help them to avoid trying to think, say or do things to make themselves better than others when they are not. Born Again Christians know that as human beings they are ordinary people and are not classed as higher as or better than other humans in this world. God created us all in the same way and Born Again Christians know that he loves us all in the same way as each other. One person is not loved more or less than another person. Born Again Christians understand that boasting about God's word (the bible) is absolutely fine because God wants them to and it is going to hopefully help non-believers convert to being Born Again Christians eventually but boasting about anything else is not. Born Again Christians understand that humbleness and humility is also part of preventing them having pride in what they do. They also know that during their lives humbleness and humility is also going to help them when doing good deeds for others and not expecting anything in return or any kind of reward for doing it. They are doing it in God's name and do it to show love towards the person or people the good deed was done for. Humbleness and humility will play a big part of a Born Again Christians life and will help them more and more as time goes by. The more humbleness and humility people have in themselves the better and Born Again Christians know that their lives are made easier because of their humbleness and humility. Doing good deeds for others becomes part of their nature and daily lives and they don't mention it anyone to gain any reward either.

Non-believers and people who are not Born Again Christians, and are not likely to be, will be not understanding or accepting God's Grace and have very little or no idea of humbleness and humility. Boasting about things other than God's word (the bible) will become natural to them including doing good deeds and expecting something in return or thinking they are better than other people for one reason or another. At the end of the day they are all human beings and part of the same world we all live in and God created. Doing bad deeds (sinning) and trying to gain from it will also prevent non-believers having humbleness and humility in themselves. This will also include burglaries and taking things from others to make a profit. Satan (The Devil) will be trying as hard as possible to prevent people from having humbleness and humility in their lives and very often they have no idea, and they fall in to same trap on a regular basis throughout their lives. It is unfortunate for them. Non-believers can very often think that because they have a job in authority that they have the right to tell anyone what to do but they can easily let their authority take over their lives and it can get out of hand. Satan (The Devil) wants them to think they have the right to order people about or tell others what to do but unfortunately in God's world they have no rights to. Authority on earth will very often lead humans in the wrong direction and will also prevent them having humbleness and humility. This is due to thinking they are in charge and that it gives them the right to be above everyone else.

Being a Born Again Christian my humbleness and humility means a lot because it means I have no rights in life to tell others what to do or to order other people about. When I go about my daily life I am all for helping people whether it is my parents, other family members, friends or neighbours, and I expect nothing in return. Doing good deeds for others becomes natural to me and it makes me feel better and makes me feel good because it has made the person's life, who I did the good deed for, a bit easier. Because God's Holy Spirit is with me continuously and his love is with me all the time things become easier including expecting nothing for doing something. That means I don't expect any rewards for what I do for others. I am one of God's children and with Jesus Christ sacrificing his life for me I take that as being very important because it means I am filled with love together with humbleness and humility. I am no better or higher than any other humans in this world and don't expect to be, whatever the reason maybe. I have no authority over anyone either. Any achievements I have had during my life have not been boasted about nor do I expect them to be. I have had various volunteer roles during my life and whatever they have included I have done them to help out the people, club or organisation I am volunteering for. I am doing it for free, to help others and because I enjoy it as well. The humbleness and humility I have in me will be with me forever as I have eternal life. Having humbleness and humility in me as part of God's Grace is a wonderful thing to be given and I am both very thankful and grateful for them both. Without them in my life things would be very different and it would let the unfortunate presence of Satan (The Devil) in to my life. Satan (The Devil) maybe trying his hardest to prevent me from having humbleness and humility in my life but he is eventually going to fail. God is in control all the time.

CHAPTER 40

Communication

Communication is a big part of all human's lives and as Born Again Christians understands and accepts God's Grace they know that God wants them to have good communication all the time including with him. God's Holy Spirit is with them throughout their lives and will be guiding them to have good communication as well. Born Again Christians not only talk to God throughout their daily lives but through praying to him on a regular basis as well. Born Again Christians as God's disciples require good communication to spread his word and to be able to speak to non-believers when explaining God's word (the bible) and when they are sharing their faith with other Born Again Christians. To be able to explain things in detail and to be able to get others to understand what has been said requires good communication including having to explain it more than once. To have good communication and to be able to explain God's word (the bible) is all part of God's Grace but is all worth it, however many times it is explained. The difference between good and bad communication could be the difference in a non-believer in becoming a Born Again Christian or staying as they are. Communication to a Born Again Christian is very important because God not only wants them to have good communication but to be able to convert a non-believer in to being a Born Again Christian and would be a massive thing. The difference between being with God or being with Satan (The Devil). Born Again Christians also have good communication when it comes to listening as well. Whether they are communicating with non-believers or other Born Again Christians, listening is very important. It may include educating people but with God's Holy Spirit guiding them, Born Again Christians are able to speak to and listen to other people at any time. God the Father, God the Son and God the Holy Spirit (the Trinity) are in continuous communication 100% of the time and forever.

For non-believers, communication is not the same. Not understanding and accepting God's Grace means communication with God is going to be virtually non-existent. Talking to God and praying to him for people who are not Born Again Christians will not be the same because their thoughts and words will not be communicating to him in the same way as people who are Born Again Christians do. Their souls will not be the same and how they talk and pray to God will not be genuine or they will mean something entirely different to what God is expecting to hear. For most non-believers and people who are not Born Again Christians communicating with people who are Born Again Christians will not be easy. Listening to a person explaining what God's word (the bible) means and accepting it will be very hard. It may include asking questions but for a non-believer to accept what they have been told by a Born Again Christian it won't be easy. Most people who are non-believers don't realise that when they are trying to communicate with God or trying to listen to a Born Again Christian's explanation of God's word (the bible), it is Satan (The Devil) who is preventing them from understanding it or having proper communication. Satan (The Devil) will be trying as hard as possible to get non-believers to forget about God and make them think that whatever they think, say or do doesn't matter, and that will have a huge effect on how they communicate with others, in particular God and Born Again Christians. Having no soul plus a bad attitude and feelings in life will also have a big effect on not being able to communicate with God or listen to Born Again Christians. If non-believers still want to be with God, then they need to genuinely communicate with God and listen to Born Again Christians because Jesus Christ could return at any time.

I myself am communicating with God every day. I say regular prayers at night times before I go to sleep and I say occasional prayers during the daytime. I also think of and talk to God at other times as well. I am always praying for his Holy Spirit to continuously guide me throughout my life. God is in control of me and I am so glad he is. I am one of his children and the communication between us has been going for a long time. I have eternal life so the communication between us will carry on forever, on both earth and in Heaven. The communication between us is so good it will never end and whatever is happening in my life God is guiding me in the right direction and will heal me when I need healing. The communication between God and I is continuously working including when he healed me of both epilepsy and bowel cancer, and during all those years he filled me with inspiration, strength, motivation and determination to keep going. Through my faith in him and accepting the gift of his Grace the communication has been there all the time. Jesus Christ is my Saviour and because Jesus Christ is God the son (part of the Trinity), I am in communication with him as well. Jesus Christ is God and is listening to my prayers and knows when I am talking to him. He sacrificed his life for me because of my sins and is listening to me when I am asking for forgiveness, plus he also knows when I am doing my job as one of his disciples and trying to explain to non-believers about what he did for me and the rest of the world. My personal communication with non-believers is when I am explaining to them about God and what Jesus Christ did for us but if they don't believe me I don't give up on them and pray for them, and hope that for their own sake they convert to being a Born Again Christian. I am unable to and wouldn't want to force anyone to believe in God but at the end of the day the decision of whether they want to believe or not is up to them.

CHAPTER 41

Body, Soul & Spirit

All human mankind is made up of body, soul and spirit. Human mankind are not just body, or just soul or just spirit they are a combination of all of them. God created each of us all in his image to be a combination of body, soul and spirit. Born Again Christians know their bodies from their souls and their spirit, because they know they were created by God and are his children as well. Born Again Christians know that their body, soul and spirit are all as important to them, as each part is part of their lives. One part cannot work without the others. To live our lives, we need a body, our bodies need a soul and within us God fills us with his Holy Spirit. Born Again Christians know that during their daily lives each one of their body, soul and spirit works with each other and that they communicate internally. Body, soul and spirit are so important to people because they are their lives. Through God's Grace people have been given them to live their lives and live how God has planned. God's Holy Spirit is guiding everyone during their daily lives and Born Again Christians know that during their lives God wants nothing but the best for them. Having God's Holy Spirit in them means their souls will be working continuously and showing their true feelings towards God and all human mankind. All human mankind's bodies when created are flesh and bones plus the essential organs, senses and personalities as well. They are just as important to be able to live a life and to Born Again Christians they are exceptionally important.

For non-believers and people who are not Born Again Christians understanding the meaning of body, soul and spirit will be very hard. Not accepting and understanding God's Grace will be one disadvantage as they will not realise that their lives are body, soul and spirit. Their bodies, as for Born Again Christians, are created by God the Father and will be the same. God also wants them to be filled with his Holy Spirit and be able to have souls but unfortunately they won't be. Because Satan (The Devil) exists he will be trying extremely hard to invade their lives and prevent them from having God's Holy Spirit in them, and that will make a huge difference to their lives. Unlike Born Again Christians, non-believers will struggle to have a soul because Satan (The Devil) will prevent them showing their true feelings. With God's Holy Spirit being rejected and their souls not working as they should, the body, soul and spirit in them will not be in communication with each other. During their daily lives their behaviour, speech, reactions and how they go about their lives will show. If people have no feelings for others, use bad language towards other people, think they are out to gain by being greedy or are intending to harm others during their lives then unfortunately Satan (The Devil) will have taken control of them and their body, soul and spirit won't work together or even exist at all. That is exceptionally sad and it will be of no good to any non-believers and people who are not Born Again Christians. Human mankind whose body, soul and spirit are not in communication with each other are going to find life much harder and also much harder to convert to being a Born Again Christian as well. People who are not Born Again Christians will not realise that their body, soul and spirit are not in communication with each other during their daily lives because Satan (The Devil) is trying exceptionally hard to prevent them from having God in their lives.

I know as a Born Again Christian that my body, soul and spirit are in communication with each other throughout the whole of my life. God created me and provided me with my body, he filled me with his Holy Spirit and the body God provided me with has a soul. Through God's Grace I have been provided with body, soul and spirit and I am so thankful and grateful for them. During my daily life and in everything I am involved in God's Holy Spirit is working in me all the time, and at the same time God's Holy Spirit is working on my soul. The soul I have and God provided me with helps me throughout my life when showing my love towards others when doing things such as saying prayers, doing good deeds to help people out, trying to make others' lives easier etc. My body, soul and spirit will be doing whatever God wants me to and whatever he is guiding me to do. I know that Satan (The Devil) will be trying his hardest to prevent my body, soul and spirit being in communication with each other but fortunately for me and because of God's power and strength in me he will eventually fail. Knowing that my body, soul and spirit are in communication with each other all the time is a wonderful feeling and wonderful to know. It means it makes my life easier even when I am going through hard times. God's Holy Spirit fills my body with many good things including strength and determination, and his Holy Spirit is also telling my soul what to think and how to feel in situations when I am with other people or when I am on my own. His Holy Spirit also keeps my soul in control and keeps me calm and relaxed. During the fifteen years I was affected by the pain and agony after being diagnosed with bowel cancer God kept me calm and relaxed all the way through. This included when I was first told of the bowel cancer and when I had a twisted colon.

CHAPTER 42

Presence

To Born Again Christians the presence of God is so important in their lives and part of God's Grace is to be present in Born Again Christians lives. God is present in the lives of Born Again Christians all the time, he is inside them and outside them wherever they maybe, whatever they are doing and whatever situation they maybe in. God is present in Born Again Christians whatever they are thinking, saying or doing. The presence of God in Born Again Christians makes life so much easier for them including making them more relaxed and less fearful. God's Holy Spirit is not only present in Born Again Christians but God's Holy Spirit is with them to guide them and make life much easier. The feeling of God's presence to Born Again Christians is a massive comfort and blessing. Born Again Christians know that they were created by God, as was the heavens and earth, and knowing that and having the presence of God in their lives makes them closer to God. God's presence in Born Again Christians lives makes their friendship with him stronger as well. God's presence in Born Again Christians also makes it easier for them to keep thinking of him during their daily lives, it also helps them when praying to him. God's presence also helps them to know he is listening to them when they are praying. God's presence in Born Again Christians also helps them with their faith, trust and belief in him.

A strong faith in God means that Born Again Christians know that during their lives God is not only present in them but they can feel him in them and it lifts their spirits throughout lives. Having God's presence in them also means that Born Again Christians know that when they sin (thought, word or deed) they know that they need to say sorry, ask forgiveness and repent from their sin(s)

For non-believers and people who are not Born Again Christians, thinking of God's presence means nothing because their thoughts and feelings are being diverted elsewhere by Satan (The Devil). During the lives of non-believers and people who are not Born Again Christians they have no idea or feelings of God's presence and don't want to either. It is a massive disadvantage to non-believers and people who are not Born Again Christians because of not wanting to have God present in their lives. They either have no idea of or want to ignore the fact that God created them and is present in this world at this very time. Because Satan (The Devil) has control over non-believers and people who are not Born Again Christians he is preventing them knowing and feeling God's presence in their lives. Satan (The Devil) is also creating bad and evil in non-believers and people who are not Born Again Christians, most don't realise it, and that will also help those people to be as far away from God as they possibly can. Having no feelings for or towards God and not realising he is present and part of this world is going to make life very hard for non-believers and people who are not Born Again Christians. Unlike Born Again Christians, people who are non-believers and people who are not Born Again Christians will not realise they can be seen and be heard by God throughout their lives but unfortunately for them they won't believe it and it means nothing to them. Having no faith, belief and trust in God will also have a big effect on not knowing or feeling God's presence. God's Grace is a gift and God's presence is part of that but for non-believers and people who are not Born Again Christians they are turning away from it, ignoring it and rejecting it, which is very sad.

For myself, as a Born Again Christian, God's presence is not only with me all the time but he is living in me, around me and with me forever. He is that close to me I am that grateful to him for his presence and the gift of his Grace. He lives with me every day and I can feel him with me as I go through my daily life. His Holy Spirit is guiding me every day in everything I do and am involved in and that gives me continuous hope and inspiration. I know that when I say my prayers God is listening to them and that he knows I am genuine and sincere in what or who I am praying for. God's presence also makes my life easier because my faith, belief and trust in him is getting stronger and stronger as time goes by. God's presence also has an effect on my friendship and closeness to him as well. I have been through various experiences in my life including forty years of epilepsy and fifteen years of cancer but during all those years God was still present in my life. I have also been through many years of unemployment and just like the epilepsy and cancer God was present in my life as he still is. There is never a second in my life where God is absent from my life because he is there all the time. God's Holy Spirit is not only present in my life and guiding me throughout my life but he is there to support my thoughts, words and deeds. The power and strength in God's Grace is not only working continuously in me and keeping my strength, positivity, determination and motivation going but it is also present in me throughout my life. Whatever happens in my life, whether I am going through good or bad experiences, God is present in my life and is with me to get me through whatever that experience is. God is also present in me when I am studying his word (the bible) and he is guiding me more and more so that I can understand his word. God is present in me when I am trying to magnify his word (the bible) to other people.

CHAPTER 43
Beauty & Nature

As well as God creating the heavens and the earth and human mankind he also created beauty and nature. This includes flowers, plants, trees, rivers, lakes, seas, oceans, animals, birds, weather etc. Beauty and nature are a big part of God's creation and a big part of life, and it all comes from his Grace. Born Again Christians understand that beauty and nature are a big part of their lives and are necessary as well. Weather includes sun and rain but without them things such as plants, flowers and trees wouldn't grow and some include growing the food we consume each day. Some animals provide the food we consume as well. Other animals are a big part of human mankind's life, some of them pets and some farm animals. Birds are also a big part of beauty and nature, and some of them include birds that provide food for human mankind. A good majority of human mankind care for and respect beauty and nature in particular Born Again Christians. They know it is through God's Grace that beauty and nature is created. Animals get fed regularly and flowers and plants get watered regularly including with the help of rain. Some birds get fed regularly and some feed themselves. Animals including fish, reptiles, mammals and other creatures usually feed themselves. Because of God's Grace and his Holy Spirit in them Born Again Christians have a good understanding of how to treat beauty and nature plus they know that beauty and nature is as important to God as human mankind is because he created all. Some humans are very attached to beauty and nature and to some it is a passion as well. Plants, flowers and trees are exceptionally important to some people, and animals and other creatures are important to other people.

For people who are non-believers and not Born Again Christians, and not likely to be, their idea of beauty and nature won't be the same as Born Again Christians. Some people who are not Born Again Christians maybe farmers, gardeners, meteorologists, scientists plus people connected with horticulture and maybe passionate about beauty and nature in one way or another. Their understanding and idea of God's creation of beauty and nature may not be the same though. There are also other non-believers and people who are not Born Again Christians who don't care for or respect beauty and nature at all. Not feeding animals, not caring about them, ill-treating and harming animals, not feeding and watering plants and flowers, plus ill-treating plants and flowers are some examples of people's whose intentions who don't care about beauty and nature. Not feeding, watering or generally caring for beauty and nature could mean killing it/them or letting it/them die, whether it be intentional or unintentional. Unfortunately for them Satan (The Devil) will not only be invading their lives but will also be putting bad thoughts and ideas in to their minds and wanting them to not care for and ill-treat beauty and nature because it is his plan. The more it happens Satan (The Devil) will not only be pleased but it is going to happen more and more because the people who are not caring for and ill-treating beauty and nature don't realise it is the plan of Satan (The Devil) tempting them in to doing it. They are falling for it and unlike Born Again Christians have no thought and love for the beauty and nature God created and all through his Grace. Harming beauty and nature will be as much a sin in God's eyes as what harming human mankind is. Some non-believers, when harming beauty and nature, are not even thinking about it being created by God. Due to Satan (The Devil) being continuously with them it will be hard for non-believers and people who are not Born Again Christians to realise that God's creation of beauty and nature is as important as his creation of human mankind.

Although my knowledge of beauty and nature is not perfect, as a Born Again Christian, my understanding of how to treat beauty and nature, and how important it is because God created it, is not too bad. God created my body and he created beauty and nature as well, so both are as equally important to God because he created us both. When I need to look after plants and flowers I will. As for feeding animals, I fed a couple of cats in my early life but since then I have not had any animals or worked with animals in my life so far. I know that because God's Holy Spirit is with me throughout my daily life he is guiding me and will be making sure that I do no harm to beauty and nature, and will be telling me that beauty and nature is as precious to him as I am. I understand as a Born Again Christian that whatever kind of weather we get we have to accept and have no control over. Animals, birds, plants and trees also mean a lot to me because I understand that as well as being part of beauty and nature they all produce food and some of them drinks as well. As a Born Again Christian and part of human mankind I need to consume a certain amount of food and drink to survive during my daily life. I am very grateful and thankful to God the Father for his creation of beauty and nature because it is a big part of my life as much as it is of other people's lives. Whether it is human mankind or beauty and nature I would treat them all equally and want them all to be loved by myself just as much as God loves me. Beauty and nature will always be an essential part of my life as is many other people's lives.

CHAPTER 44

Sacrificing Life

For Born Again Christians, Jesus Christ sacrificing his life means everything to them because if he hadn't both they and the whole of human mankind would have had no second chance of being able to live a perfect life in Heaven when he returns. Jesus Christ sacrificing his life is all part of God's Grace and is exceptionally important because it is possibly the biggest part of God's plan for human mankind to be living a life that he promised when he first created the heavens and the earth together with mankind. Born Again Christians understand and accept God's Grace and know that Jesus Christ sacrificing his life for them is a big part of their daily lives. In sacrificing his life, it makes Jesus Christ Saviour of the world and for Born Again Christians it means more than anything to them. There are many things that Born Again Christians pray for and all these prayers are said through Jesus Christ Saviour of the world because of his sacrifice of his life, and all for human mankind. Human mankind, whether they are Born Again Christians or not, all sin and virtually every day. Born Again Christians recognise the majority of their sins and do also ask forgiveness either instantly or at a later time. There are sins they don't recognise, more likely bad thoughts, but they still ask for forgiveness when saying their prayers. Born Again Christians know that it is all because of Satan (The Devil) that Jesus Christ sacrificed his life on the cross, because if Jesus Christ hadn't sacrificed his life for the whole of human mankind there would be no possibility of living a perfect life in Heaven. If Satan (The Devil) hadn't existed and caused temptation and the beginning of sin/evil Jesus Christ wouldn't have needed to sacrifice his life on the cross. Born Again Christians also know that it is only through the sacrifice of Jesus Christ on the cross that they will be able to enter Heaven and live a perfect life.

For non-believers and people who are not Born Again Christians, and are not likely to be, knowing and understanding what Jesus Christ's sacrifice for human mankind is all about, will be very hard for them. Not having accepted or understanding God's Grace will make it harder as will not accepting or wanting the know Jesus Christ (God the Son – part of The Trinity). Because Satan (The Devil) is working on non-believers and is preventing them from having faith, belief and trust in God, that will also continuously make them ignore who Jesus Christ is and what he has done for them and the whole of human mankind. They will continue to disbelieve and not accept that Jesus Christ sacrificed his life for them and the whole of human mankind, and that it was all because of the sins they have committed during their lives. Satan (The Devil) will also have enough power to make non-believers not realise that because they have no belief in Jesus Christ's sacrifice for them that it will mean Satan (The Devil) taking control of them. It will also mean it will be exceptionally hard for them to accept who Jesus Christ is and what he has done for them. Some non-believers who have completely no intentions of believing in God have no idea where they are going to end up when Jesus Christ returns. It is exceptionally sad for them but included in God's Grace is his justice and that is going to be very important. God will also know who has faith and who doesn't plus he knows who believes, understands and accepts what Jesus Christ's sacrifice for human mankind means. Non-believers will not only need help but also need some guidance from a Born Again Christian to realise that Jesus Christ saved their lives and that they need to convert to being a Born Again Christian.

As a Born Again Christian, Jesus Christ sacrificing his life for me means such a lot. My belief, faith and trust in him is continuous throughout my daily life. I know that Jesus Christ sacrificed his life for me because of my sins and because he wants me to live a perfect life in Heaven. He is also shining on me and is the light of the world. If Jesus Christ hadn't sacrificed his life on the cross for me I would have had to live in a world that included much evil caused by Satan (The Devil) forever and for eternity. Because of Jesus Christ sacrificing his life on the cross for me and my belief, faith and trust in him as a Born Again Christian I have a second chance of living a perfect life in Heaven where there will be no evil at all. It means because Jesus Christ sacrificed his life for me it means his love for me is 100% perfect and the friendship because of what he did for me is there all the time. The sacrifice Jesus Christ did for me is something exceptionally special and will continue to be so. The fact that Jesus Christ sacrificed his life for me fills me with hope, delight, happiness, strength and motivation. It also fills me with so much positivity and optimism as well including the time when I had my life saved when I developed bowel cancer in 2000. God really did use his power and glory to save me from the bowel cancer and for me to overcome the fifteen years of pain and agony, and that gave me another chance to be one of Jesus' disciples and carry on spreading his word to as many people as possible. I was also given that chance to be one of Jesus' disciples because he sacrificed his life on the cross for me. If anyone asked me what is the best thing in my life, I would tell them that is was Jesus Christ sacrificing his life for me on the cross.

CHAPTER 45

Conquering Death

Through God's Grace, Jesus Christ's birth and resurrection includes conquering death. Born Again Christians know that through Jesus Christ's sacrifice on the cross and because he rose again he has conquered death, and that means Born Again Christians will be living eternal lives on earth and in Heaven as well. When a Born Again Christian's body stops functioning on earth they don't die because their soul and spirit goes with them to Heaven where they join God. This will only happen if a Born Again Christian's body stops functioning before Jesus Christ returns. If a Born Again Christian is still living their earthly life and Jesus Christ returns their bodies will rise up with him and change from being an imperfect body in to a perfect body. Conquering death is not only important but it was never part of God's promise and plan to have death at any time. Death only exists due to the presence of Satan (The Devil) because of the evil and sin that exists in the universe, whether it was in the past, the present or in the future. Jesus Christ's birth and resurrection was all part of God's promise and plan because he knew that Satan (The Devil) would be coming and that he would be causing evil and death in the world. God's Grace and love for all of mankind meant that things were supposed to be perfect including a perfect world, no deaths and no harm either. Death was never supposed to exist when

God created the universe. Born Again Christians are not only thankful but also very grateful that Jesus Christ has conquered death through his resurrection because they will be living a perfect life with a perfect body, which is also part of God's promise and plan.

People who are not Born Again Christians, as well as not understanding and accepting God's Grace will also not realise that through Jesus Christ's sacrifice on the cross it means that they would be saved and living in a different world with a perfect body. Because Satan (The Devil) has control over people who are not Born Again Christians he is putting thoughts and feelings in to them including making them think that if their actions during their daily lives include sinning, harming another human or killing another human that it doesn't matter at the end of the day. He is also making non-believers think that death is just part of life and that it has to happen at some time and after that there is nowhere to go anymore. He is trying to give them no hope, be negative and think that after death it is the end of the world. More and more people who are not Born Again Christians are not realising that because of Jesus Christ's sacrifice on the cross he has conquered death. That doesn't mean a thing to people who are not Born Again Christians because their understanding of what Jesus Christ did for them and for all of human mankind doesn't exist. Satan (The Devil) really is and will be taking control of people who are not Born Again Christians and that will certainly get in to them that death hasn't been conquered. Having no faith, belief and trust in God will not only make it harder but Satan (The Devil) will be trying as hard as he can to make non-believers think that death has to exist at some time and that it is impossible for it to go away.

As a Born Again Christian, I know that for me, Jesus Christ has definitely conquered death because I will be with God in Heaven whether I am still living my earthly life and Jesus Christ returns or my body stops functioning before he returns and my soul and spirit joins him in Heaven when I start living a new life with a new body. That body will be a perfect body. If Jesus Christ hadn't conquered death and Satan (The Devil) got his way, the universe would have been filled with sin and death forever. I wouldn't have been able to be saved or been given a chance to live a perfect life in Heaven with a perfect body. Jesus Christ conquering death means so much to me because through God's Grace and my faith, trust and belief in him I will be able to live a life in Heaven, which is what God promised me and planned for me. What it means to me and knowing that I am saved makes me feel and know that Jesus Christ conquering death is not only very important but it means the difference between knowing that I will be living in Heaven rather than living in Hell. For me, the difference is massive. Living my life in a place with a body which is 100% perfect is that good I can't ask for anything more, and this is all through Jesus Christ conquering death. Otherwise, I would have been living in a place which is 100% evil with an imperfect body as well. Jesus Christ conquered death for me and as a Born Again Christian I know that he saved me because he doesn't want me to have an imperfect body or live in an evil world forever. I don't want an imperfect body and I know that only Satan (The Devil) is the one who has caused me to sin at any time. God knows that through my prayers I have asked for forgiveness and repented from my sins. Through Jesus Christ conquering death and saving me it means my life in Heaven will be completely sin free. While I am living my life on earth and knowing that Jesus Christ conquered death on my behalf makes me feel so good and it is also in my thoughts and feelings as I go through my daily life. It is hard to forget when it means so much.

CHAPTER 46

Freedom

God's Grace, as well as being a gift from him, also gives all of human mankind the freedom to have faith, belief and trust in him. God created all human mankind and we are all able to make decisions and all have a choice as well. Born Again Christians have a choice and they have made the correct decision because they have chosen to have faith, belief and trust in God. As well as having faith, belief and trust in God he has sent his Holy Spirit to guide Born Again Christians and keep on giving them freedom to carry on making the correct decisions. For people who are Born Again Christians they are not only thankful but also very grateful to God because he gave them the freedom to have faith, belief and trust in him. That means being saved and living eternal life on earth and in Heaven. When God created all human mankind he promised and planned to give them the freedom of the universe. That also meant living perfect lives and having perfect bodies. Unfortunately, the presence of Satan (The Devil) prevented that. As well as God's Holy Spirit guiding Born Again Christians during their daily lives that also includes giving them the freedom to make choices and the correct choices. The prayers that Born Again Christians say to God will also give them freedom to make the correct decisions. When Born Again Christians enter Heaven they will have complete freedom because life in Heaven will be perfect as will their bodies. During their earthly lives Born Again Christians have the freedom God gave them but as their lives and bodies are imperfect due to Satan (The Devil) things will be a bit harder for them although they will still be able to overcome that problem.

For people who are not Born Again Christians freedom will mean nothing to them. The problem is that they have no idea and don't realise that Satan (The Devil) is in control of them and taking away the freedom that God promised and planned for all human mankind, and also putting bad thoughts and feelings in to them to make them make the wrong decisions during their daily lives. In doing this, Satan (The Devil) is filling people who are not Born Again Christians with as many reasons and restrictions to not have faith, belief and trust in God and that will make them reject God's freedom. This will include all the various rules and restrictions other religions have, some include one form of punishment or another. Having those rules and restrictions are all part of sinning and going against God's word, and are not part of freedom either. People that live their daily lives with all these rules and restrictions on top of them are not only living a life without freedom but they are also going to have a very hard life as well. All these rules and restrictions within various religions come from Satan (The Devil) because he wants to prevent them from having freedom and put as much evil and hatred in to their lives as he possibly can. Some non-believers are actually convinced that their religions are correct, even without freedom, but unfortunately they will find out they have done wrong when Jesus Christ returns. People who are of no religion at all will also not understand the meaning of freedom because of not understanding or accepting God's Grace. Although they have the freedom to make decisions during their daily lives, unfortunately for them it will be the wrong decisions. Having freedom taken away from them will prevent non-believers from entering God's world and will eventually lead them in to entering Satan's (The Devil's) world in Hell.

As a Born Again Christian, being with God continuously makes me feel wanted and I know that he is giving me the freedom to believe in him or not, and his Holy Spirit is guiding me to make the correct decisions. Sometimes Satan (The Devil) causes me make the occasional incorrect decisions during my life. I have to ask for forgiveness and repent from them. The freedom I have to live my daily life is important plus I know that it all comes from God because he created me. God wanted me to have freedom when he created me because freedom is all part of his Grace and has no attachments, restrictions or rules to prevent anything. As a Born Again Christian I have complete freedom compared to those of other religions who are ruled or restricted to what they can say, do and believe in. My life is made so much easier with the freedom God is giving me. God's promise and plan is for me to live with the knowledge and feeling that I can live in complete freedom during both my earthly life and when I enter Heaven because I am saved. Because I have been given complete freedom by God it makes it so much easier for me to relax, stay calm and feel his love and friendship towards me. Because I am currently living my life on earth I still have an imperfect body but as I am a Born Again Christian God knows that as well as being saved and being one of his disciples I have no intentions of restricting or making rules to prevent other human beings living their lives. I want other human beings to live their lives without additional restrictions and rules and live a life of complete freedom. The difference between living a life of rules, restrictions and being trapped by Satan's (The Devil's) evil plans compared to living a life of complete freedom is massive. I am actually praying and willing God's Holy Spirit to keep guiding me throughout my life because that will also give me freedom forever. I am exceptionally grateful to God for my freedom and I will make the most of it.

CHAPTER 47
Sanctification & Consecration

As part of God's Grace he wants the whole of human mankind to receive sanctification and consecration. Born Again Christians know that during every human being's earthly life complete sanctification and consecration isn't possible. Due to the presence of Satan (The Devil) no human being can be completely sanctified and consecrated during their earthly life. Born Again Christians will be receiving sanctification and consecration throughout the whole of their daily lives and will accept it all the time. God's promise and plan is for the whole of human mankind is to be completely sanctified and consecrated. Born Again Christians know that because they have imperfect bodies during their earthly lives that God's sanctification and consecration for them is extremely important and necessary. Born Again Christians know that the only way their imperfect bodies can be made perfect is through Jesus Christ' birth, sacrifice on the cross (resurrection), rising again and his return. When Jesus Christ returns and Born Again Christians enter Heaven they will have been completely sanctified and consecrated, and they will have perfect bodies. With the presence of Satan (The Devil) during mankind's earthly lives no human beings can be completely cleansed or healed. Because all human beings have imperfect bodies during their earthly lives and God's promise and plan is to see them have perfect bodies they need to be cleansed and healed (sanctified and consecrated). With their faith, belief and trust in God, and through their saviour Jesus Christ, Born Again Christians will eventually be sanctified and consecrated. God knows that without the presence of Satan (The Devil) sanctification and consecration wouldn't have been necessary. For Born Again Christians, receiving sanctification and consecration from God is exceptionally important to them because the difference between having an imperfect body and a perfect body is massive. Born Again Christians also know that God is trying his hardest to sanctify and consecrate them during their earthly lives and they pray for it as much as possible.

For people who are not Born Again Christians, and have no intensions of being so, receiving sanctification and consecration from God will be virtually impossible. Having no faith, belief and trust in God and not wanting to accept and understand his Grace will have a big effect because Satan (The Devil) will be preventing them from receiving sanctification and consecration. The presence of Satan (The Devil) will prevent non-believers being sanctified and consecrated, and will make their imperfect bodies during their earthly lives stay as they are and because they have no faith, belief and trust in Jesus Christ the Saviour, when he returns their imperfect bodies will actually get much worse because they will be joining Satan (The Devil) in Hell. The amount of evil that Satan (The Devil) is spreading around the world is just impossible to imagine but people who are not Born Again Christians are letting him take advantage of them and will make God's sanctification and consecration for them be impossible. Jesus Christ was born, sacrificed his life on the cross for them, rose again and will return again but unfortunately for people who are not Born Again Christians that will be of no benefit to them because they will be rejecting all of that and will be unable to be sanctified and consecrated. They have no idea of what it means and don't realise that as well as Satan (The Devil) taking control of them and due to not wanting to believe in the Lord that sanctification and consecration for them will be impossible. People who are not Born Again Christians would be better off getting help and advice from a Born Again Christian before they make a terrible decision. If they convert to being a Born Again Christian, people that were non-believers would start accepting God's Grace and would eventually be able to receive sanctification and consecration. God's sanctification and consecration for all of human mankind through Jesus Christ is to make their imperfect bodies become perfect but non-believers are rejecting this. Rejecting it is a sin because God is going above and beyond to give all human beings a perfect life.

As a Born Again Christian I want God's sanctification and consecration for me to continue forever because as I have an imperfect body at the present time and throughout my earthly life, I want that to change. The only reason I have an imperfect body is because Satan (The Devil) exists and is trying to prevent me being sanctified and consecrated by God. Fortunately, he will eventually fail. I know that because Jesus Christ was born, sacrificed his life for me, rose again and when he returns, I as a Born Again Christian will join him in Heaven. In joining Jesus Christ in Heaven my body will be new and completely sanctified and consecrated. God's sanctification and consecration of me will have been completed. At the present time I am living my earthly life and throughout my daily life I know that I have an imperfect body due to sinning and health issues etc. God's promise and plan for me wasn't to have an imperfect body so I need to be cleansed and healed throughout my daily life. As God is in control of this universe I am going to let him sanctify and consecrate me as much as he can and use all the power he has to provide me with the best life I can live. I know that as part of his Grace he will sanctify and consecrate me because he wants the best for me and wants me to eventually become fully sanctified and consecrated and have a perfect body. God's sanctification and consecration of me is extremely important to me and I am extremely thankful and grateful, and to my saviour Jesus Christ for giving me the chance to live a new life in Heaven and to be completely sanctified and consecrated. The difference between the life I will be living in Heaven, with a completely sanctified and consecrated body, is going to be extremely different to the life I am living on earth at the present time.

The changes are going to be unimaginable plus indescribable and I for one am really looking forward to seeing when I am fully sanctified and consecrated. I continue to pray for God's sanctification and consecration of me and that he keeps on cleansing and healing me throughout my daily life.

CHAPTER 48
Magnifying & Magnification

When God created the universe including the heavens and the earth plus all human mankind he expected and wanted all human mankind to magnify his name by spreading the word. God the Father, God the Son (Jesus Christ) and God the Holy Spirit (The Trinity, also known as God the three-in-one) need to be magnified. Magnifying/magnification are also part of God's Grace and Born Again Christians understand that they need to magnify our Lord as much as possible. There is no limit to how much we can magnify our Lord. The more magnifying our Lord we do the better. Born Again Christians understand magnifying our Lord to other people because God is in them all the time, throughout their lives, and they are intending to magnify their Lord as much as they can. The response they get when magnifying their Lord to others is varied and is up to the person who is listening and possibly responding. The gift of God's Grace gives Born Again Christians a massive advantage when magnifying God's word to other people because they know God is with them continuously and God's Holy Spirit is guiding them all the time. Born Again Christians are not only studying God's word (the bible) but what they are studying is also being retained in their mind and soul. How Born Again Christians go about magnifying God's word to others is up to them and there are various ways of going about it and the closer to God they are the easier it becomes. Magnifying our Lord is the best thing Born Again Christians can do because they are letting others know that God the Father created the universe they live in, God the Son (Jesus Christ) died on the cross for them because of their sins and God the Holy Spirit is guiding them, as long as they believe, trust and have faith in him.

For people who are non-believers and people who are not Born Again Christians, magnifying God's word is virtually impossible because their problem is that Satan (The Devil) is with them all the time and they don't realise it or they don't have any feelings about God's word. Very often non-believers and people who are not Born Again Christians are not likely to want to listen to Born Again Christians who are trying to magnify God's word to them. Unfortunately for non-believers and people who are not Born Again Christians they are not studying God's word (the bible) and will not be able magnify God's word to anyone. Satan (The Devil) is trying his hardest to prevent non-believers and people who are not Born Again Christians magnifying God's word or even understand it, and he is succeeding with them. The more Satan (The Devil) gets his way with non-believers and people who are not Born Again Christians, the more likely they are to magnify bad and evil to people that don't need it in their lives. Because non-believers and people who are not Born Again Christians are not receiving the gift of God's Grace they have a massive disadvantage in life because they can't or won't have any feelings towards or for God (the Father, the Son or the Holy Spirit) and won't be able to receive magnification of God's word from people who are Born Again Christians.

The presence and power of Satan (The Devil) in people who are non-believers and people who are not Born Again Christians is going to too much for them to have anything to do with the magnification of God's word (the bible). If people who are non-believers and people who are not Born Again Christians want to be saved, they need to start having belief, faith and trust in God and then they need to start receiving magnification of God's word (the bible) from Born Again Christians.

For myself, as a Born Again Christian, I am happy to magnify God's word (the bible) to anyone. Whether they want to listen to me, respond, ask questions, start learning or studying it, or start believing in God themselves, is up to them. When I first started attending church services in the early 1980's other Born Again Christians were magnifying God's word to me which helped me a lot. I attended church services, house groups (bible studies), Alpha courses etc. God's Grace is will me all the time and God wants me to use the Grace I have been given to magnify his word (the bible) to others. How they react is up to them. When I have magnified God's word (the bible) to others in the past, some have completely ignored me, some have said they need proof of God to believe in him, some have listened and asked a few questions, whether any have become Christians due to my magnification of my Lord's word (the bible) I don't know. As time has gone on I have got closer to God and my faith, belief and trust in him has got stronger and stronger, and that has helped me enormously with my magnification/magnifying of my Lord's word. For me, being able to magnify God's word (the bible) is a wonderful thing because it is the best thing a Born Again

Christian like myself can do. When I magnify God's word (the bible) to anyone, how they respond or deal with that magnification of the Lord's word, could be the difference between having a life in Heaven with God and having a life in Hell with Satan (The Devil). During my earthly life God's Holy Spirit is not only with me all the time but is guiding me when I am magnifying his word to other people. The feeling of God's Holy Spirit being with me and guiding me throughout my life is a wonderful feeling and I know God's Grace and love is with me all the time. As one of his disciples, the more people I am able to magnify God's word (the bible) to the better. The magnification of God's word (the bible) can get people thinking and whether they start to explore and read about God's word (the bible) it is up to them and will be very beneficial because of where their lives will be when Jesus Christ returns.

CHAPTER 49

Promises & Plan

When God created the universe including the heavens and the earth plus all human mankind he had promises and plans to provide all human beings with perfect bodies and perfect lives. Born Again Christians know that although God is continually trying to sanctify and consecrate all humans the reason they can't have perfect bodies and lives is because of the presence of Satan (The Devil). Through their faith, belief and trust in God, through his Grace, Born Again Christians know that although Satan (The Devil) is preventing God's promises and plans happening during their earthly lives. That is only temporary because when Jesus Christ returns God's promises and plans will all take place when Born Again Christians enter Heaven. Jesus Christ was born, sacrificed his life on the cross for all Born Again Christians, rose again and will return again, and is the only way God's promises and plans will come true. Born Again Christians are not only willing and praying to God for him to sanctify and consecrate them but also that his promises and plans will take place and come true but they know it can't happen until Jesus Christ their saviour returns. God's promises and plans are an important part of a Born Again Christian's life because it is their life and because they are his children as well. Because God's promises and plans are for Born Again Christians to have perfect bodies and lives it means so much to Born Again Christians plus they are exceptionally thankful and grateful. It all comes from his Grace for all of human mankind.

Although God's plans and promises are for human mankind to have perfect bodies and live perfect lives, for people who are not Born Again Christians and have no intentions of being so, God's promises and plans will not end as they should do. Because Satan (The Devil) is trying his hardest to ruin and destroy people's lives that means as well as trying to fill people with sin and cause as much bad and evil as possible, he is also destroying the promises and plans God has for human mankind. Unlike Born Again Christians, non-believers will not want anything to do with what God's promises and plans are because they have no faith, belief and trust in him and have no idea of what Jesus Christ has done for them. Because of the evil that Satan (The Devil) is putting in to those who are not Born Again Christians, who have no faith, belief and trust in God, God's promises and plans for them will be non-existent. It is not only exceptionally unfortunate for those who don't accept and understand God's Grace because as well as affecting them a lot it will put them under the complete control of Satan (The Devil) who will eventually prevent them from knowing anything about God's promises and plans for them. They will actually find out what promises and plans Satan (The Devil) has for them in Hell. It is very hard to imagine a person having a life in Hell compared to Heaven, and if only they had faith, belief and trust in God and understood what his promises and plans for them were.

As a Born Again Christian I understand that God's promises and plans for me include having a perfect body and a perfect life but as I have the presence of Satan (The Devil) during my earthly life that isn't possible. I know that because Jesus Christ was born, sacrificed his life on the cross for me, died, was buried, rose again and will return for me, he is the reason God's promises and plans for me will still come true. I may have been through forty years of epilepsy, fifteen years of bowel cancer and long periods of unemployment but my faith, belief and trust in God, through his Grace, will get me through my earthly life and will help me to face any other battles I happen to face in the future. I am not only excited but looking forward to the day Jesus Christ returns and I enter Heaven because God's promises and plans for me will have come true. All of this is part of what I have been studying through God's word (the bible). Although God's promises and plans for me is to provide me with a perfect body and life throughout my life I know that although Satan (The Devil) has prevented that, he will eventually fail, because it is only going to be temporary. God created me, he knows my body, soul and spirit, and through his Holy Spirit is guiding me all the time. One of God's plans for me since the invasion of Satan (The Devil) is to sanctify and consecrate me through his Holy Spirit and keep me under control. I pray for this to happen all the time. Because of Satan (The Devil) it means God's promises and plans for Born Again Christians have been put on hold until the return of Jesus Christ, when everything will go back to how it should have been originally. God's promises and plans for my life were planned a long, long time before I was actually born. God promises and plans are not only wanting the best for me but as well as providing me with a perfect body and a perfect life he is going above and beyond to see that his Holy Spirit helps me to know how to live a Christian life, know how to spread his word like a disciple, know what his friendship means and know that Jesus Christ is the light of the world. As well as it being a free gift to the whole of human mankind God's Grace includes everything that a human being would need to live the kind of life that God promises and plans them to have, and everyone should understand it and accept it because it is more powerful than anything they could want. As one of Jesus's disciples I would like to say to everyone in this world and make it clear to everyone that you have all been given a chance to understand and accept the gift of God's Grace, study his word (the bible), and live a life as a Born Again Christian. The power of God's Grace certainly works.

www.ingramcontent.com/pod-product-compliance
Lightning Source LLC
Chambersburg PA
CBHW071431070526
44578CB00001B/72